Praise for
The Surfman's Daughter

Enjoyed by adults, teens, families

In eight charming and poignant vignettes, Rebecca Locklear evokes life in the sweet and harsh Chatham of over a century ago....

—*Debra Lawless, author of* Chatham in the Jazz Age

Delightful, true stories with wonderful historical and everyday life detail.

—*Alice Reader, editor*

Fabulous presentation of life at the time.... It's interesting to know what life was like for a kid: chores, dangers, expectations. Charming stories that leave you wanting more.

—*John Chamberlain, author of* Finding Things (A Joe Martin Novel)

The Surfman's Daughter explodes with information you've never even considered...along with meaningful and engaging discussion topics.

—*Carol Smathers, university faculty*

If you like *Anne of Green Gables*, you will enjoy these true-story cameos of Roxane—mischievous, bright, and full of fun!

—*Beth Lambright, historical speaker/reenactor*

Each chapter is filled with personal stories that reflect life in the early 1900s when people lived without electricity, provided their own food, and their transportation was by horse or boat. *The Surfman's Daughter* provides students with many hands-on activities. A must-read for all who love to learn about history through literature.

–*Susan Reed,* Homeschool Life Magazine

A girl's life is beautifully portrayed in these thought-provoking glimpses into an oft-forgotten past.

—Celia Martin, author of A Bewitching Dilemma

You feel like you're really there on the seashore, living that life of struggle, family connection, and support.

—Linda Jones, educator

I like these stories very much. They're a window into a gentle, loving family in a much different America from now.

—David Greenberg, author of A Tugging String

My only request is that I want more stories! This is a peek back into a little-known part of our history through a first-hand account. Roxane is so REAL. My family was drawn to her because of her hilarious exploits.

—Jenny Underwood, educator

The Surfman's Daughter

A short-story biography
of Roxane Eldredge's early life

1904–1929

*A surfman was a member
of the U.S. Life-Saving Service (1878–1915)*

REBECCA LOCKLEAR

Skaket Books and Art

The Surfman's Daughter

Publisher's Cataloging-in-Publication Data

Locklear, Rebecca—author.
The surfman's daughter: growing up in a Cape Cod village 1904-1929 / Rebecca Locklear.
Redmond, OR: Skaket Books and Art, 2022. | Includes bibliographical references.
LCCN 2021924607 (print) | ISBN 978-1-7335915-8-4 (paperback) |
  ISBN 978-1-7335915-9-1 (ebook)
LCSH: Eldredge family. | Massachusetts—History—20th century. | Massachusetts—Biography. | Lifesaving—Massachusetts—Cape Cod—History. | Chatham (Mass.)—History. |
  BISAC: HISTORY / United States / State & Local / New England (CT, MA, ME, NH, RI, VT) | BIOGRAPHY & AUTOBIOGRAPHY / Historical. | BIOGRAPHY & AUTOBIOGRAPHY / Women. | HISTORY / United States / 20th Century.
LCC F72.C3 L63 2022 (print) | LCC F72.C3 (ebook) | DDC 974.4—dc23.

The Surfman's Daughter

Copyright © 2022 Rebecca Locklear
Map, schooner, ornament illustrations © 2022 Ven Locklear
Ernest S. Eldredge homestead illustrations © 2022 Jack Dolan
Front cover photo © Christopher Seufert Photography
Photos used by permission.
Book cover and interior formatting: Melissa Williams Design
Publisher: Skaket Books and Art skaketbooksandart@gmail.com

Notice: The information and details in this book are true to the best of the author's knowledge. Nevertheless, the contents are offered without guarantee. The author and Skaket Books and Art disclaim all liability to any party in connection with the contents or use of this book.

All rights reserved.
No part of this book may be reproduced, stored, put on the internet, or transmitted in any form or by any means without prior written permission from the publisher. Brief quotations are allowed in articles and reviews.

COVER PHOTOS: Roxane Eldredge c. 1926
              Harding's Beach, Chatham, Cape Cod, Massachusetts

Dedicated to

Descendants of
Ernest Sanford Eldredge and
Mehitable Gould Eldredge

History-loving cousins who descend
from Roxane Eldredge's ancestors:

William Eldredge, Revolutionary War patriot
William and Anne Nickerson, founders of Chatham, Massachusetts
William Brewster, Stephen Hopkins, John Howland,
Thomas Rogers, and John Tilley, Mayflower passengers

and to
Barbara Eldredge Stevenson

Contents

Map of Chatham, Massachusetts 1900	10
Introduction, Eldredge Family	11
Prologue: Outhouse *1909 Roxane, age 5*	13
Saturday Treat *1909 Roxane, age 5*	15
The Cold Fire *1910 Roxane, age 6*	24
My Beautiful Pink Sweater *1913 Roxane, age 8*	37
Sprayed *1913 Roxane, age 9*	53
PHOTOS	61
The Pianist *1919 Roxane, age 14*	72
The Finish Line *1922 Roxane, age 17*	84
Out Fishing *1929 Roxane, age 25*	92
Epilogue: Family Bios through 1929	101
Extra Story: A Voice that Called *1961 Roxane, age 56*	104
Notes	109
Sources, List of Illustrations	114
Acknowledgments, Final Thoughts	118

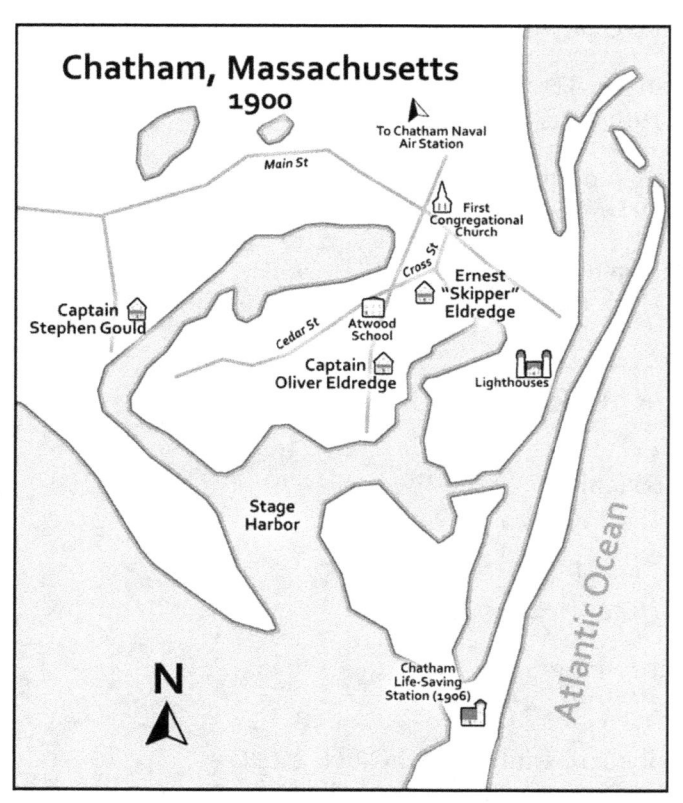

Introduction

- Do you wonder what it was like to live back in the days before computers, electric lights, electric washing machines and dryers, indoor running water, and indoor bathrooms?
- Can you envision having to provide your own food? This could include hunting and fishing, having a milk cow and chickens, as well as growing and canning vegetables and fruit. How difficult was it to cook on a stove that burned coal or wood?
- What would it have been like to walk to everything within a five-mile radius or to travel farther mainly by horse and cart, or boat?

Roxane Eldredge grew up in that era. She was born in 1904 in the fishing village of Chatham, Cape Cod, Massachusetts.

As an adult, Roxane entertained guests with stories and remembrances from her childhood and years as a young teacher. She also shared stories about her sea-faring ancestors for nearly thirty years when she served as a docent at the Atwood Museum in Chatham. It wasn't until 1991 that Roxane spent a year and a half writing her recollections in a small 44-page journal, focusing on incidents that shaped her life. Part of that journal, along with personal letters and postcards, photo explanations, family interviews, and in-depth research, combine to accurately portray events in this book.

This early biography of Roxane, revealed through stories, provides a glimpse into the early 1900s while addressing mistakes, loss, perseverance, and love.

Eldredge Family

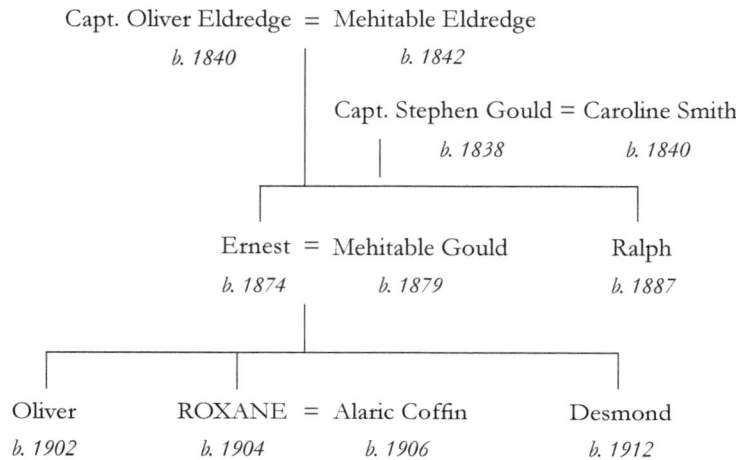

Ernest Eldredge Homestead 1904

Prologue

Outhouse

October 9, 1909 ~ Roxane, age 5
Chatham, Cape Cod, Massachusetts

A grunt and beastly holler stopped Roxane and Oliver in their tracks. The deepened dusk made it difficult to identify the dark shape advancing toward them.

"Who's that?" cried 5-year-old Roxane as she tugged on her brother's sleeve. They were nearly back to their house after playing with neighbor children.

Oliver pulled Roxane with him behind the nearest tree. "Stay hidden," he whispered.

Roxane tucked her skirt between her knees and stood still.

Peering around the trunk, Oliver scanned the homestead. "Looks like the Reverend. Comin' from the outhouse."

Roxane gasped.

"Now he's at the back door. Mother's coming out, wringing her hands on her apron like she does." He paused. "Hear him yelling? He's rightly mad." Oliver shook his head. "Doggonit. By the way he's rubbin' his backside, I bet he got his bum pecked."

"But Oliver," Roxane whined in a hushed voice, "they dared us to throw chickens down the three-holer. We had to do it! We had to!"

"Maybe." Oliver turned to Roxane and continued in an underbreath. "We didn't count on the Reverend comin' for a visit. He's stomping down the drive. Wait 'till he passes three houses."

Roxane felt shivers climb up her legs as she cast an anxious glance toward the sandy street.

Looking down into Roxane's large brown eyes, Oliver raised his eyebrows and made an obvious pronouncement: "Now is not the time to go home."

THE END

Saturday Treat

November, 1909 ~ Roxane, age 5
Chatham, Cape Cod, Massachusetts

The dory cleaved through the dark ocean water and emerged from a light fog. Ernest Eldredge, known to all as "Skipper," approached the shore at Stage Harbor with speed and skill. As the craft's bow rose out of the water and came to rest on the sand, he settled the oars to the side. Six feet tall and thin as a rail, his height was in his legs, as they say. Using those long legs, he jumped neatly over the side, pulled up the boat, and tied it to an anchor secured in the sand.

At age 35, Skipper was in his eleventh season as a surfman with the U.S. Life-Saving Service, a shore-based search and rescue agency.[1] The August through May season covered the time when most shipwrecks and strandings occurred. He and six others lived and worked at the Chatham Life-Saving Station on an isolated barrier beach. Today was his *liberty day*, or day off. Starting at 11:30 in the morning, he had 24 hours to be home with his wife Hittie and their two children.

"Skip! Skipper!"

Skipper looked up to see his youngest brother striding over from the fishing fleet area. "You going out?" he called to Ralph. "Mackerel?"

Ralph Eldredge, at 22, was a top-notch fisherman. "Nah. Was doing a couple of repairs and knew you'd be comin' in if the fair weather held." He rubbed his cold, gloved hands together. "I'm done for the season. Will find some other work this winter."

Eager to get home, Skipper set a brisk pace along the marshy shore. Above them rose a grassy hill, topped by the old grain windmill his grandfather had owned. He glanced over at Ralph. "You could apply as a surfman substitute for the winter. You have the strength."

Ralph, a head shorter than Skipper and stout, hurried to keep up. "There's a sense of comfort having you at the Chatham Station. But look," Ralph pointed out, "I get enough rough weather as it is. And, Lordy, it's blasted cold. When a storm approaches, mine is the first boat back at the dock. Then it's home for me with Mother's stew and biscuits." He shook his head. "When I think of your crew pulling that 900-pound surfboat through the sand upwards of a mile and then launching it into the surf, why, that's brutal."

"We hitch a horse to the boat these days."

"But you didn't used to," countered Ralph. "You're tough. Rock-solid. I wouldn't have the stamina."

They turned down Atwood Street. "You remember my first day on the job," Skipper remarked. "The Blizzard of '98. We set out at sunset to assist the *Fairfax*. I thought it my first trip out and my last.[2] But I've gone out so many times now. Don't sell yourself short, Brother," he said reassuringly. "You're as strong as the rest of us."

"But it's more than strength and you know it." Ralph adjusted his knitted cap. "Not everyone has the mental fortitude for boring beach duty, punctuated every now and then by the sheer terror of rescues."

Skipper slowed. "To fight nature . . ." he reflected.

Ralph interrupted. "And we're talking the hurricane-type nature."

"To fight nature and rescue people. To save a soul." He shrugged. "If I can, I must."

"I still say you fellows go where no sane man would ever go. Speaking of going," he said, changing the subject, "are you off to town tonight? Frank's bringing the last of the ice cream for cones down at church."

"Wouldn't miss it," Skipper admitted. "Don't know when I'll have another Saturday night off. I'm for ice cream. Good stuff."

Ralph smiled. "I'll meet you at church. After supper."

As they cut across the field near the parental homestead, Ralph chuckled at the thought of his niece. "I was just thinking that Roxane takes after you, Skip. If you shave off that mustache, you'd see she has the same mouth and nose as you. Forget the looks, though. What I'm saying is that she jumps right in the water, so to speak."

"Gets in trouble."

"True enough," Ralph admitted, "but she has spunk. Determination, I'd say. And she's only five."

Skipper shook his head and smiled. "She and the other small fry put a cat in my tool chest last week. I was about to fix the cart."[3]

"See? She even pulls jokes like you do. You hate cats! She's quick-witted, that one." Speculating, he added, "I can just see her rowing out in a storm."

Skipper stopped. "No way," he said sharply.

"Don't give me that command voice. I'm not saying for real. But she's fearless. Mark my words," he said with confidence, "the older she gets, the more she'll keep you on your toes, right enough."

The brothers parted. Ralph turned down the long driveway to the sprawling family home while Skipper continued to his own two-story farmhouse on Cross Street, taking the porch steps three at a time.[4]

That evening, after supper

Roxane and Oliver dashed for the stairs to see who could reach their bedroom first.

"Ice cream!" Roxane yelled, as she grabbed the bannister railing and scrambled up after Oliver. "Wait for me!"

The family had just finished their Saturday night supper of fish and baked beans when Skipper announced they would walk to town for ice cream cones. But first, they had to change into their nice clothes.

Looking over at his wife, so pretty with her thick brown hair wrapped in a bun, Skipper smiled. "Thanks for supper, Hittie. It's good to be home. Fowl or fish stew we make at the station can't compare with your cooking." He snuffed the cluster of candles in the center of the table and rose. "Ralph plans to meet us. Let's leave shortly."

Hittie began gathering dishes to set in the kitchen. "You like watching the children jump up and down with excitement."

"Indeed." Taking one of the kitchen lanterns, he followed the children upstairs and set it on the table at the top of the stairs so a bit of light would slide into the three darkened bedrooms.

Roxane scooted around her four-poster bed and the doll furniture her dad had built from cranberry crates. "Where's my sweater?" she whined. "It was on the trunk." She tried to open the armoire but gave up and scrambled onto her bed.

In his room at the front of the house, Oliver shrugged into a clean shirt. With his round face and blue eyes framed by thin eyebrows, his sleepy-eyed look belied his considerable energy. While tucking in his shirt, he hurried to Roxane's room. "Don't worry. Mother will be right up."

Bouncing up and down on her knees and setting the bed to creaking, Roxane blurted out, "I love ice cream! Ice creeeeeam!" She bounced and bounced, her shoulder-length brown hair whipping out behind her.

Oliver joined in, bouncing and laughing. "Remember to say *thank you*."

"I will. I will!" Roxane beamed.

"Here comes Mother." Oliver slid off the bed and went back to his room.

Hittie helped Roxane into a nice dress and buttoned her navy blue cardigan. "You'll get a quick spit bath when we get home. Go see what Oliver is doing for a few minutes."

Having changed into his civvies, the only suit he owned, Skipper lazily descended the stairs, pausing on the upper landing, then sliding his hand along the smooth, thick banister. It was only five years ago that he had built the house and he was proud of it. In the spacious country kitchen, with a lantern creating dancing shadows, he chose the bench tucked against the far wall near the pantry to sit and stretch out his legs. He always had trouble sitting in regular chairs with his long legs.

Soon, Hittie joined him, setting her lantern on the table. "I'm ready."

Skipper looked toward the hallway that led to the stairs and shouted, "Oliver! Roxane!" As he stood, one of his trouser legs briefly remained stuck to something on the bench. Twisting around, he pulled his pant leg away from his thigh and scowled. "What the dickens?"

Oliver and Roxane bounded into the kitchen but stopped at the outraged expression on their father's face.

"Who stuck the glob of gum on the bench?" he demanded. Long strands of gum ran from the bench to his good suit pants. Bits stuck to his fingers as he tried to pick it off the fabric. Drawing up to his full height, he folded his arms across his chest and glared at the children.

Roxane looked over at Oliver for some backup, but he just raised his eyebrows and said nothing. There was no way to get out of it. "I did," she stammered, looking at the floor.

"Oh dear," Hittie uttered, as she set a lantern next to Skipper. "I will try, Skip." She shot a look at Roxane. "I already know Wrigley's Spearmint is difficult to get out of clothes."

Skipper strode out of the kitchen to go change. No one spoke as Hittie cleaned up the mess.

When he returned, Skipper's command was stern. "Roxane, come here." He took her hand and walked into the parlor, prepared to give her a spanking. "Never do that again, Roxane. Never put gum anywhere but in the wastepaper can. I am spanking you so you will remember this." After the spanking he continued. "There will be no walking to town tonight."

Roxane scooted up the stairs to her bedroom and flopped on her bed.

A few minutes later, Oliver poked his head into her room. "Sorry about the spanking," he whispered.

She sat up, tears running down her face. "I don't care about being spanked," she burst out indignantly. "It doesn't hurt at all," she lied. She flopped back on the bed. "I don't get my ice cream! I want ice cream!"

Downstairs, Skipper took up his coat and hat. "Hittie, I'll check the animals." Under the darkened sky, he made his way down the cart track to the barn.

Hittie shook her head. *He's like a strong wind. Restless. Direct.* A few minutes later, she heard a loud knock on the back door.

"Hello!" Ralph called, as he walked in. "I was comin' down the street, expecting your house to be totally dark like the others, but I saw a light on. Everyone else is already down at church. Ready to go? I'm a bit late myself."

On her knees, rearranging items in the icebox, Hittie turned. "Ralph." She shrugged, resigned.

Oliver rushed in for a hug. "Uncle Ralph!"

Ralph's eyes twinkled. "So ice cream doesn't interest you, huh? Just hanging around here?"

Oliver became serious. "Roxane parked her gum right there." He pointed to the spot on the bench. "Dad sat on it. She got a spanking."

Ralph nodded. "Oh-ho. I see clearly. Say no more." He turned to Hittie, as she made her way to the sink. "Why don't I stay here with the rascal while the rest of you go to town?" he offered.

"Thanks, but the decision's been made." She started on the pile of dirty dishes with a sigh. "We're not going. Might as well retire early."

Ralph turned back to Oliver. "Looks like you're disappointed too, squirt."

Oliver nodded, looking glum.

Always optimistic, Ralph raised his eyebrows. "Sometimes we are disappointed, but you know? Keep a lookout for snow. Snow ice cream can't be beat. Remember that. Now," he said, "I have time for one game. What will it be? You choose and bring it here."

Oliver brightened like a struck match and made a beeline to the parlor.

"Thanks, Ralph," Hittie said. "I made an apple pie for Skip. He's at the barn. A slice? Hot cocoa?"

"You know I can't refuse food. Thanks."

Oliver slid onto a kitchen chair with a deck of playing cards in his hand.

"You know Oliver, at this time of year we men prefer hot cocoa and apple pie. Your mother has just the thing."

"I'll be back in a moment, Ralph. Need to check on Roxane." Hittie strode toward the stairs.

Oliver tilted his head. "Are you going to tell everyone?"

"You mean about Roxane and the gum?" Ralph pondered a bit. "The word will probably get out. As for me, I'm mum as an oyster." *Oh yes, Skip*, Ralph thought to himself. *Roxane will keep you on your toes, right enough.*

THE END

Conversation

1) In these stories, the first names of Roxane's parents are used for clarity. At that time however, adults were always addressed either by their surnames or by familiar names like Mom, Uncle Jim, or Grandpa Smith. Why did society start allowing children to address adults by their first names? Why are last names rarely used except for teachers, doctors, or politicians? Do forms of address have to do with respect or are they more for identifying people?

2) If Skipper was home on a Saturday night from his work at the life-saving station, the family would dress up and go down to Frank Kelley's Ice Cream store during the months it was open. At age 87, Roxane recounted the gum story in her journal, adding, "What a sad night. I have never cared for gum since!"[5] Share a time when you did something wrong unintentionally.

3) Iceboxes were a bit like refrigerators, but much smaller. Cooling was supplied by a block of ice which had to be replaced at intervals. The Eldredge's icebox looked like a wooden chest (29x18x30) with a typically small space at the bottom to store food. Discuss what it would have been like to plan and prepare meals with limited refrigeration.[6]

4) Being spanked was common in the 1900s. When reflecting on her childhood, Roxane wrote this: "I deserved every spanking my father gave me and I'm glad that he spanked me very hard. Somehow, I felt it made me a better person. At least I knew that he loved me enough to spank me. It showed that he cared."[7] What disciplinary methods are used successfully today?

5) Like other men of his time, Skipper was the unchallenged head of his household. He made decisions and had the last word. He trained his children to obey without question, dispute, or delay, and to tell the truth. It was up to him to mete out punishment. How do you think surfman-husbands fulfilled this responsibility when only home one day each week? What occupations today take the father or mother from their families for extended times? How do these families manage parenting responsibilities?

Doing

Research: During the 1800s, trade along America's coastal states was done mostly by sea. The peak of the trade was between 1870 and 1910, when thousands of ships sailed up and down the coasts with cargo. In November 1909, surfmen at the Chatham station recorded (during daylight hours) 33–52 schooners, sloops, steamers, or barges-in-tow every day.[8] Unfortunately, bad weather, along with a lack of navigational aids and communication, led to numerous strandings and shipwrecks. Look up the sinking of the RMS *Republic* on January 24, 1909.

Ice Cream: Ralph Eldredge mentioned eating snow ice cream. The next time it snows, gather clean snow into cold bowls, then spoon hot maple syrup on top to make a gummy topping. In the 1930s one writer made this comment: "Served with plain doughnuts, hot coffee, and sour pickles, there is little to compare with the tasty simplicity of snow ice cream."[9]

The Cold Fire

Saturday, October 1, 1910 – Roxane, age 6
Chatham, Cape Cod, Massachusetts

Grabbing the polished wood banister at the top of the staircase, six-year-old Roxane jumped three stairs at a time, her nightgown billowing behind her, and landed at the bottom with a smile. After Saturday chores, she was free to climb trees, go down to the pond, or just tag along with her brother.

Her mother Hittie was at the kitchen sink, cleaning up from preparing seafood stuffing and setting fish to soak in milk. "Good morning, dear. Why don't you get your brush?"

A few minutes later, while Hittie brushed out Roxane's wavy hair, Roxane started squirming in the chair. "Are you doing wash today?" She hoped to get that chore done as quickly as possible.

"No, dear, I'm not planning to wash. I'll wait 'till next week. Dad will be back by then and I'll have his clothes. He had midnight beach duty last night, looking for ships that are too close to land. But poor Dad has double duty."[10] Quizzing Roxane she asked, "What time will he get back to the station?"

"Eight o'clock."

"Exactly. That's right about now." Feeling they all needed a break from work, she added, "It's such a glorious day, why don't you and Oliver walk to Grandpa and Grandma's?"

"We can go to Grandpa's!" Roxane shouted, as her mother finished with her hair by pulling the front strands into a side barrette.

Oliver must have heard her when he came through the back door, his hands still wet from a quick wash outside. A broad smile made it clear he loved going to Grandpa's house.

Hittie turned to Oliver. "Are the animals fed? Stalls cleaned?"

"It's done." Oliver slid into his chair at the kitchen table, pulled a warm biscuit from the basket and reached for the grape jelly. Hittie had cut his hair into a bowl-shape and with his round face he looked like an angelic choirboy.

"Before you leave, Oliver," Hittie added, "I need another bucket of coal to keep this fire going. And would you grab the towels off the line? I need to do some baking but will meet you at Grandpa's for lunch. Let him know I'll be at the shore at noon."

⁓

On their walks, sometimes Roxane and Oliver ventured off the sandy road to investigate a bird or some animal, but most of the time they stayed on the road. To pass the time, Oliver quizzed Roxane. "What kinds of shellfish do we have?"

"Quahogs and steamers. Oysters. Mussels."

He looked over at Roxane. "That's all?"

"Oh yeah, and razor clams."

"And scallops," Oliver added.

Roxane had her own question. "Why do waves turn white after they flip over?"

After passing the Atwood School and continuing the length of Cedar Street, they came to Oyster River where they could see right across to Grandpa Gould's oyster shanties in West Chatham.

Oliver cupped his hands around his mouth and gave a holler. "Grandpa! Grandpa!" He counted to ten. Two more times he gave the call. That was the signal. They sat down on the bank to wait.

In a few minutes, their grandpa, Captain Stephen Gould, emerged from a shanty and waved. Moving to the dock, he untied a skiff, and with deliberate strokes rowed across the river to his grandchildren.

After settling in the boat for the short ride, Roxane looked around and realized why she loved this place. Shanties lined the shore where her grandpa had his oyster business.[11] Behind the sheds, mounds of blindingly white oyster shells melted into grass-covered hillsides. Grandpa said that every last tree had been cut years ago. Now all she could see was white and green sandwiched between the blue of the river and sky. Reaching over the side of the boat, she let the cool water run through her fingers while the breeze played with thin strands of her hair. She straightened up to absorb the familiar, distinctive smell of the salt marsh.

Once on land, Roxane hugged her grandpa around his waist. She knew he was old and moved slowly, but she loved him. He was the one person who understood her eagerness to know everything.

Captain Gould ruffled Oliver's hair. "Go find Gram now. Go on. Off with you," he ordered in his stern captain's voice. "Both of you!" He spoiled the effect though with a wink and a smile.

Roxane raced Oliver across the littered oyster shells, every step a crunch, then circled some wooden barrels and lobster traps before the final burst of speed up the hill. The central chimney of the shingled, three-quarter Cape house beckoned them to its hearth-warmed kitchen.

Oliver got there first. "Gram!" he yelled, as he burst into the house.

"Well, bless your hearts!" Caroline Gould leaned down for hugs and gave each a kiss on the forehead.

"You must be hungry after your walk. Just sit right down." Caroline bustled about while the children sat at the kitchen table. From the dark pantry she brought out honey cakes along with butter from the icebox.

Roxane got up. "I'll help you."

"Thank you, dear." She gave Roxane a small jar of milk to put on the table and sat down with them.

Oliver bit into a honey cake. "Would you tell us the molasses story again?"

Caroline put her hands on her hips, her smile framed by dimples. "Are you telling me you don't like those honey cakes?" She poured milk into their glasses.

"No, no! I mean yes, I like the honey cakes!"

"Here's the story. Your grandpa and his crew used to sail to New Orleans with barrels of salted codfish and other Cape Cod products. After selling the fish, he'd buy sugar and barrels of molasses. Then he'd sail back here."

"He sold the molasses for ten cents a quart, right?"

"That's right, Oliver, and that's making good money. On one trip, Grandpa asked me to go with him." She stood to get more milk from the icebox. "That was when I was young and full of pep and vinegar," she added, over her shoulder.

Setting the jar on the table, she continued. "One day, while we were still in Louisiana, Grandpa needed to go ashore alone. Since I had to stay on board, I sat on deck and watched men unload goods at the docks. There were some colored men stomping around barefoot in wooden vats and I wondered what they were doing. Later, I asked Grandpa why the men were stomping around. He told me that they were stomping the sap out of sugar cane to make molasses."

Oliver smiled. "So you don't eat anything with molasses in it."

"Nothing," replied Caroline. "I don't like the thought of someone stepping in my food."[12]

Roxane imagined how fun it would be to squish her toes in the thick gooeyness of it all. "What about baked beans with a little bit of molasses?" she asked.

"Not even baked beans with molasses."

Oliver took another drink of milk. "In the winter, Mother gives us a spoonful of sulfur and molasses every morning. It's awful."

"But sulfur and molasses does keep you in good health. Other people use molasses and no one seems to get sick. I just don't want to eat it."

Roxane folded her hands politely in her lap and gave a quirky little smile. There was no way she would ever give up eating her mother's molasses cookies.

At noon, Captain Gould rowed across the river to pick up Hittie for lunch. Back at the house, he made an announcement. "I have a grand idea. Roxane, would you and Oliver like to spend the night with us?"

Roxane jumped up and down and clapped her hands with delight. "Yeah!" Sleeping on feather beds was like being wrapped in comfort.

Her joy was short-lived.

Hittie turned the cup of tea in her hands. "Father, I don't think they should stay here tonight." She hesitated, not wanting to offend her parents. "It's now October and it's kind of chilly." She turned to Oliver and Roxane. "Grandpa and Gram don't have a coal fire."

"*Cold* fire?" Roxane asked.

"At home we have a coal fire that will keep you warm."

It wasn't clear to Roxane what her mother meant by a *cold* fire, so she soon forgot about it. However, off and on that afternoon she teased her mother to let them stay overnight. Sometimes her sweet smiles got what she wanted. Not this time.

In the late afternoon, after a row across the river, the three of them headed home, much to her disappointment.

The next day, a fine Sunday morning, Hittie let Oliver and Roxane play *Puss in the Corner* on her big bed while she went downstairs to get a fire going in the black iron kitchen stove. On the nightstand at the head of the bed, she kept a kerosene lamp and a dish of matches. Pasted to the cover of the dish was a bit of sandpaper so she could strike a match and light the lamp.

While they were playing the game, Roxane kept getting into the corner near the nightstand. Several times she glanced over at the matches in the dish. She knew she shouldn't touch them, so she turned to Oliver. "Please light a match."

"Mother said to never touch the dish."

"Please, Oliver. I just want to stick my finger in the fire to see if it's hot or cold."

"It's hot."

"I just want to know for myself. Mother said yesterday we have a *cold* fire. Didn't you hear at Grandpa's? She said fire is cold."

Oliver slid off the bed, grabbed Roxane's shoulders and looked in her eyes. "No. Mother says not to touch matches. Never to touch matches. Anyway, there's no such thing as a *cold* fire." He released her. "Now, this time you be *Puss* and I'll start in this corner."

"Come on, Oliver. She'll never know. Dad always says you learn things by doing them."

Oliver finally gave in to her pleading, as she knew he would. "Oh, all right." He went over to the dish of matches and scratched a match on the cover. Roxane stuck her finger in the blazing fire and indeed, it was hot. They blew on the match, thinking it was out, and threw it on the plank floor.

A few minutes later, after finishing the game, she sat down in the same area where they had thrown the match and sucked on her lightly burned finger. Gradually, the floor got hot. Roxane scooted back closer to the bed and held her breath. "Oliver," she squeaked nervously. "Oliver?"

Oliver was lying on the bed, staring at the ceiling and feeling a bit guilty. "Roxane, I know I shouldn't have lit that match." *I know what's right and wrong.*

Licks of flame appeared in the cracks of the floorboards. "Oliver! The fire!" Roxane's eyes widened with fear as she clambered onto the high bed. As she turned back to look way down at the floor, it took her a moment to realize the bottom of her flannel nightgown was on fire. She screamed, scrambling to the head of the bed on top of the pillows. "Get off! Get off!" she yelled at the fire. Grabbing her nightgown, she shook it, trying to get the fire away.

In a few seconds, her nightgown was burning furiously and so was she.

"No!" Oliver shouted, as he fumbled to gain footing on the big bed. "Mother!" he yelled. By then, Roxane was flailing her arms wildly. Screams filled the house.

Hittie tore up the stairs. When she saw Roxane, she grabbed a quilt and rolled her in it to smother the flames. Gathering Roxane to her chest, she shouted directions at Oliver. "Throw the braided rug on the fire. Do it!"

Oliver lifted the heavy rug and flung it toward the burning floor.

"Grab the hall rug," she yelled with urgency.

He ran to the hall.

"Toss it on the other one. Stamp on it!"

Oliver hesitated.

"Stamp on the rugs good and hard!" she commanded.

He tapped at the outer edges as flames escaped near the nightstand.

"Not just the sides. Make sure the fire's out. Get it out!"

Feathers were now everywhere as pillows and bedding burned. Hittie swatted at the bed with a flannel shirt while cradling Roxane's upper body in her left arm, repeating over and over, "It's all right, it's all right. I have you. I love you."

Roxane's agonizing cries seeped through the house.

Hittie glanced at Oliver. "Is it out?"

Oliver nodded, too petrified to speak.

"Now go! Run for help!"

Weeks later

Images and voices drifted in and out of Roxane's consciousness, but she really didn't remember much for a long time after the accident. The doctor kept her on morphine for weeks and perhaps that made her mind fuzzy. She did remember one particular day when Oliver came to see her after school.

Tears were streaming down her face, the kind of tears that don't stop. Her bed had been moved from upstairs, down to the parlor where the couch used to be. Stretched out on her stomach, with her head turned to the right, she fingered the soft quilt hanging over the side of her bed.

Her gaze moved to the window where the leaves on the tree had decided not to be green anymore, then shifted to the platform rocker and down to the large braided wool rug on the floor. She knew the pattern by heart. Two black braids circled the outside of the rug. The next braid changed to two strands of black and one strand of blue. That went around the rug once. Then it was one strand of black, and two strands of blue. Round and round the braids went like the endless days spent in bed.

A slight movement brought stinging pain to her back. She winced. The doctor said the burns on her back, left arm, and under her armpit were very bad and she must lie still. She hated staying in bed. She hated her bed.

The kitchen door slammed and a light patter of footsteps made her hold her breath.

"Roxane, I brought you a book from school," Oliver called out, as he came around the corner. Seeing her tears, he stopped. "Oh, you're sad again." He sat on the chair next to the bed and brushed his fingers over her night-time braid. "You'll be all right. Remember, Mother always says to *say your prayers and eat your vegetables* and you've been doing that. You'll get better." He opened the book on a low table next to the bed. "Look at the pictures. I'll read you the story when I get back from the barn." He got up to leave.

A moan escaped from her mouth.

Oliver came back to the bed. "What does Gram always say?"

"When I breathe in my back hurts," Roxane complained, trying to talk without moving her lips.

Oliver waited.

Roxane rolled her eyes. "Count your blessings."

"Say the whole thing."

With a small huff, Roxane mumbled the verse. "Count your blessings, name them one by one. And it will surprise you what the Lord has done."

"All right. You hurt. Name something you're thankful for," Oliver demanded. "A blessing."

"You."

Silence hummed. Oliver couldn't get over feeling guilty about lighting that match.

Roxane continued. "And Mother, Dad, Grandpa and Gram Gould, Grandpa and Grandma Eldredge."

"Go on."

"My three perfect sand dollars and the white rock with specks."

Oliver jumped in. "What about peppermint sticks?"

"Apple pie."

"Ice shavings."

"Ice cream!" By then, Roxane was smiling and so was Oliver. They continued to think of other things to be thankful for: the sun, moon, skunks, muskrats, right whales, terns, the tomcat, cardinals, and the little brown bunnies out back that eat clover.

"You don't even have any chores to do," he said. "You lazy bum!"

She giggled.

Oliver left to get to his chores.

Roxane stayed on her stomach in bed and looked out the window at the pretty colors floating off the tree.

Epilogue

All through the winter, Roxane remained on her stomach. She wasn't allowed to turn over. Six months after the accident, in the month of April, the doctor came to the house and announced she was healed. Then, she got up.[13]

Due to her injuries, Roxane missed first grade. Here's what Roxane wrote many years later:

> "When I was able to go back to school [in the fall], I didn't want to be in first grade with those little kids. My mother dragged me down to the Atwood School. I cried all the way. After the morning exercises the teacher welcomed me back and said the School Committee and Superintendent of Schools, Loring G. Williams, were going to give me a month's trial in the second grade. Oh boy, was that a challenge. I made it."[14]

THE END

Conversation

1) Roxane wrote this in her journal:

   "We didn't know anything about vitamins when I was growing up. So Mother kept a pan of sulfur and molasses on the back of the stove. Each morning my two brothers and I would line up and Mother would give us each a spoonful of sulfur and molasses to get us through the cold winter. It worked quite well. If any of us had an earache, Mother would put the heart of an onion in our ear."[15]

   Share home remedies used today that work well.

2) Roxane's maternal grandmother, Caroline Gould, spoke of "colored men" stomping in vats.[16] She wasn't being disrespectful. That term was used historically to denote black people. How has terminology changed now that minorities have more of a say in the matter of self-identification?

3) In what ways do you think the Eldredge family struggled while Roxane recovered? Have you, or someone you know of, cared for an injured family member? What was that like?

4) Although Roxane specifically wrote in her journal, "I played with matches and burnt my body very badly," Oliver assumed responsibility for the accident. He would probably have agreed that the most difficult person to forgive is yourself. Think of a time when you had to forgive yourself. What stands in the way of forgiveness?

5) There was a risk of house fires when fire was used to cook, light, and heat homes. Until 1911, when Chatham established a fire department, the only way to fight a fire was with a bucket brigade. That said, houses did withstand fires. They were built of solid wood with 12 to 15-inch beams with walls of wood or plaster. Today, there are fewer house fires comparatively but they are more dangerous than in 1900, according to the Chatham Fire Department, due to light-weight construction and the use of flammable materials such as adhesives, plastics, and insulation. Apart from the actual house itself, discuss ways you can protect your home from fire.

Note: In 1920 the town of Chatham had 783 dwellings and 13 town fires.

Doing

<u>Research</u>: Roxane was on morphine for weeks. How was morphine used in 1910 prior to World War I? What are the long-term side effects of morphine use? Speculate how Roxane could have been affected.

<u>Sayings</u>: Oliver often refers to Eldredge family sayings like "Say your prayers and eat your vegetables" or "Have an attitude of gratitude." Though not exactly a saying, his paternal grandpa, Captain Oliver Eldredge (b.1840) wrote, "When we've gotten to where we know we don't know, we've just started to know something."[17] There were also regional sayings like, "I feel like a 9 with the tail cut off." Make a list of sayings from your family or write one of your own. Create greeting cards or a wall-hanging with one or all of them.

Family Seafood Stuffing: Preheat oven to 350° F.

1) Melt 3 tablespoons butter in a skillet over medium heat. Add 1/4 cup each: diced red onions and celery. Sauté 2 minutes. Add 1/4 cup clam juice and 1/4 teaspoon seafood seasoning, such as Park Hill Maple Pepper from Savory Spice Shop or Old Bay Seasoning. Remove from heat.

2) In a bowl, combine 3 cups stale, dry bread cubes, 1 beaten egg, 1/2 cup chopped raw shrimp, 1/2 cup chopped raw scallops, and the sautéed vegetable mixture.

3) Transfer to a buttered 1½-quart baking dish and sprinkle with 2 tablespoons clam juice.

4) Cover and bake for 25 minutes. Remove cover, fluff stuffing, then bake an additional 5 minutes uncovered. Scoop into seashells and serve.

My Beautiful Pink Sweater

Spring, 1913 ~ Roxane, age 8
Chatham, Cape Cod, Massachusetts

Eight-year-old Roxane pressed her forehead against the display window of Johnny Howes' dry goods store in Chatham and cupped her hands around her eyes so she could peer inside. There, draped on a simple metal frame, was a sweater. A bright pink sweater.

She stood motionless, gazing with her mouth open. She had seen plenty of pink flowers, but never a pink sweater. All the girls she knew wore brown or dark blue sweaters. She glanced down at her brown dress trimmed in white. *I would look so pretty in that sweater*, she thought. She turned and reached for the doorknob. A little brass bell announced her entrance.

Towels, sheets and yardage filled the store. Soaps exuded a clean, fresh scent. In the back corner, a small pot-bellied stove kept the place cozy during much of the year.

"Why hello, Miss Roxane," greeted Mrs. O'Neil as she stepped from behind the counter. "What can I do for you?" Florence O'Neal, Mr. Howes' daughter, ran the store with marked efficiency and a sunny smile.

"Hello, Mrs. O'Neil. There's a pink sweater in the window."

"Ah, the pink angora sweater. Would you like to see it?" Mrs. O'Neil walked to the window display and gently lifted the sweater from the frame. "Let's see if it will fit." She held it up to Roxane's shoulders. "It's a little big, but that's good because you can grow into it. It would look nice over your dress."

Roxane caressed the fuzzy material and looked up at Mrs. O'Neil. "How do they make pink? I've never seen pink."

"It's difficult to make bright colors because the dyes are not too good. That's why most people wear brown, black, or blue. That sweater arrived just this week. It's lovely."

"How much does it cost?"

"It's rather dear," admitted Mrs. O'Neil. "Three dollars."

Roxane's shoulders drooped. Three dollars was a lot of money. She watched as Mrs. O'Neil put the sweater away and felt a desperate longing. She wanted that sweater. *I'm going to figure out how to get it before someone else buys it*, she thought, as she twirled her hair in her right fingers. "Thank you for showing me the sweater, Mrs. O'Neil. I'm going home now. Bye!"

A horse-drawn wagon rattled down Main Street as Roxane stepped in and out of the shadows cast by silverleaf maples and poplars along the road. Taking a roundabout way home, she passed the big house down by Oyster Pond, glad to see dandelions in bloom. Thinking her mother would appreciate a bunch of greens, she gathered as many as she could.

After cutting through the spacious grounds of several homes, she arrived at the two-story house her father had built in 1904—the year she was born. Instead of running up the front steps to the porch and into the entry, she went around back, past the wood shed and three-holer outhouse, in search of her older brother, Oliver. She needed advice.

Tippy, the family dog, met her near the gray-shingled barn. "Hey, old boy. Were you waiting for me?" Bending down, she rubbed his head. "You were?"

Tippy looked up at Roxane with adoring eyes.

"Where's Oliver?" She pretended to hear the answer. "You say he's inside the barn? Are you comin'?" She pushed open one of the double doors. "Oliver? Are you in here?" She put the greens on top of the nearby tack box.

"Over here."

Tippy led the way around the wagon to the stall where Oliver was combing Laddie's mane. Up came the bay's head, its ears tilted forward.

"I'm glad you're here and not out on the boat. Guess what?" she began with excitement. "I saw the prettiest sweater at the store. I want it so very much." She clasped her hands to her chest. "I want it more than anything in the world."

"A sweater?"

"Yes."

Oliver stopped grooming the horse and came around to the stall door. "If you said you wanted your own clam rake, I would understand. But a sweater? Aren't you wearing one?"

"Yes, but I want a pink one. Pink!" she exclaimed, her cheeks aglow. "How can I get it? It's three dollars."

Oliver turned back to the horse, his hand sliding to the satin nose. "That's a lot of money. Why do you want this sweater?" He grabbed a different brush. "Don't beat around the bush."

"It's warm."

"And?"

Under her breath she muttered, "It's pretty. I mean, I would be pretty."

"Girls." He rolled his eyes and let out a long sigh. "If you won't ever bother me again about this, I'll give you some advice. Talk to Mother. Don't talk to Dad. Dad would never spend a penny on something you don't need, like a pink sweater."

Excitedly, Roxane clapped her hands. "I knew you'd help me." She grabbed the dandelion greens and took off for the house, Tippy running and barking right beside her.

Bursting into the spacious, country kitchen, she plopped the greens on the counter.

"Roxane, dear," Hittie whispered. "Shhh. Desmond is asleep." In the corner of the kitchen, her baby brother looked pretty cute in the crib. "I see you found some greens. Bless your heart. Now, why don't you wash up, then set the table for supper?"

Roxane grabbed a bucket and went outside to the cistern to wash her face and hands. Back inside, she counted silverware from the drawer. Taking a deep breath, she began. "I was passing by the dry goods store this afternoon. In the window was a pink sweater." She paused. "It would keep me warm and look nice over my dress."

Hittie looked up from peeling carrots. "Pink?"

"Mrs. O'Neil held it up to me and said it would fit. She said it's big enough so I can even wear it next year . . . and maybe the year after."

"Hmmm. How much is it?"

Roxane placed a fork neatly beside each cloth napkin. "Three dollars."

Hittie added vegetables and fish to the pot on the black iron stove, ran her hands down the front of her apron, then sat at the kitchen table. "Roxane," she said in a resigned voice, "we don't have the money. The blue one you're wearing is perfectly good."

"But it's not pink. What about the money I earn?" Roxane thought back to last fall when she earned fifty cents a day picking cranberries on her hands and knees. That was ten cents for each seven-quart pail of cranberries she picked. Now she worked for four hours on Saturday mornings for Mrs. Laurence Howes, changing beds, dusting, mopping, and washing cooking dishes. Every Saturday she earned fifty cents. "Do you think I could save some of the money I earn on Saturdays?"[18]

"No, dear," Hittie said kindly. "We count on the money

you and Oliver bring in. Every penny is used for food and coal."

Roxane sat down. "Maybe I could weed Mrs. Nickerson's garden when the plants start coming up."

"How can you do another job as well as your schoolwork and chores? I don't think so. Is this sweater that important?" She pushed a few strands of hair back into her bun and reached for a glass of water.

"I have my heart set on it."

The moment stretched.

Hittie stood and pushed in her chair. Taking a large wooden spoon from the crock next to the stove, she began to stir the fish chowder. "So, the sweater is three dollars. Perhaps, and I say *perhaps* if you do one extra chore around the house, we'll let you keep the money you earn for the next six Saturdays. Then you'll have enough money for the sweater. What do you think?"

Jumping up and down with excitement, Roxane hurried over to give her mother a big hug. "I'll work really hard."

"I'm sure you will. I tell you what. I'll speak with Mrs. O'Neil at the store tomorrow to see if she'd be willing to save the sweater for you. If so, you can pay her for it in six weeks."

The next day, Mrs. O'Neil said she would save the sweater for Roxane.

Six weeks later, on a Friday night

On the night before the long-awaited day when Roxane would finally buy the sweater, the Eldredge family gathered in the dining room for supper.

At the head of the handcrafted table with ornate rounded legs that Skipper had made, was a captain's chair adorned with intricate carvings in the backrest. Skipper slid into his chair. He was on his day off from the Chatham Life-Saving

Station, where he worked long hours. When a nor'easter storm blew in, ships would either try to anchor away from land or get into port. But sometimes a ship struck a sandbar and began to break apart. The crew would row out to the ship in the midst of the storm to save lives and property. He was definitely a no-nonsense kind of man.

Oliver had just brought up a jar of peaches for dessert from down cellar and slid into his seat. Roxane sat politely with her hands folded in her lap and Hittie stood with baby Desmond in her arms. Skipper recited the familiar surfman prayer as they all bowed their heads. "Heavenly Father, bestow Thy blessing. Make us truly thankful. Pardon our sins. Amen."

"Roxane dear," Hittie began, as she placed a jar of homemade sweet pickles on the table and then sat down. "Mrs. Howes told me today you've been working hard these past weeks. The beds have been well-made. Dishes have been stacked neatly in the pantry."

Skipper settled back in his chair. "I'm proud of you, Roxane. I don't see why you must have another sweater, but you accomplish what you set out to do. That's what's important."

Roxane blushed and looked down. "Thank you." She glanced up.

Oliver gave her a wink.

Hittie then had an idea. "You know, the dry goods store is open on Friday nights." She turned to Roxane. "You have two dollars and fifty cents. What if Dad and I loan you fifty cents? That way, you can get the sweater tonight. Tomorrow, after Mrs. Howes pays you, you can pay us back."

After supper, Roxane nearly dragged her mother down to the store, skipping and laughing the whole way. The brass bell jingled as they entered.

When Mrs. O'Neil saw them, she reached up to the shelf behind the counter for the wrapped package tied with twine.

"I'm so happy for you, Roxane," she exclaimed. "You'll look like a princess in this sweater!"

Instead of jumping up and down with joy like she wanted to do, Roxane acted like a lady and calmly placed her money on the counter. She felt grown up.

As they began their brisk walk back home, the package tucked under Roxane's arm, the usual evening fog began to creep inland. Roxane shivered. Had she known the impending fate of her pink sweater, she might have clutched the package more tightly.

On Saturday morning, Roxane descended the stairs and glided into the kitchen.

Hittie glanced at Roxane as she reached for some plates. "You need to save your pink sweater for Sundays and special days, dear. Go take it off."

Roxane picked out a biscuit from the basket on the kitchen table. "Can I wear it, I mean *may* I wear it over to the Howes' house? Please?" There were six Howes daughters and she wanted to show off the sweater. "I'm not going to work yet. I'll only be gone a short while."

Hittie turned and studied her hopeful expression.

"I'll be back before you have the chance to miss me."

"All right," Hittie conceded. "You may go."

Roxane darted through Dr. Minnie Buck's backyard and over to Mr. and Mrs. David Howes' home. Sophia, the eldest at age 20, answered the door.

Roxane stood rooted to the spot for a moment, always in awe of Sophia with her chestnut hair piled on her head and starched floor-length dress.

"Oh my, Roxane," Sophia exclaimed. "Look at you! Come in!"

Roxane entered regally and did a spin. "What do you think?" she asked, with a brilliant smile.

Sophia gave a shout. "Everyone! Come see Roxane."

In a few moments, Sophia's sisters Arvilla and Emma came into the parlor, followed by twins Barbara and Bathsheba and 9-year-old Josephine.

Emma was first to comment as they all felt the material. "So this is the sweater. Beautiful. I had no idea it would be so fuzzy."

"I love the way it feels," Roxane exclaimed, so proud to be surrounded by the girls and loving the attention.

Sophia just stood there. "How did you convince your parents to let you buy this? The color is perfect with your wavy brown hair."

Josephine kept stroking a sleeve. "I wish I had a sweater like this. It's so soft." The others agreed.

"I have to take this off and go to work." Roxane started for the door, then turned and clapped her hands together. "I did it! I got it!"

On her way back home through Dr. Buck's backyard, the hens and rooster there were making a racket. The last time she heard that kind of noise, a fox had managed to kill one of their own chickens and there was blood everywhere. *I know I shouldn't go into a neighbor's hen house without asking,* she thought, *but I just don't want something bad to happen.* She paused for a moment to scan the ground and didn't see anything unusual, so she ran through the gate and ducked in through the hen house door to see what was going on.

Immediately, the chickens crowded around her legs, anticipating a scattering of cracked corn or table scraps. Nothing seemed amiss, so she pushed her way through them and automatically began to search for eggs.

The second nest revealed two eggs of unusual color. She picked up those nice, warm eggs, amazed at the mixture of brown and pink. Slowly, she put them back. She picked them up again and rubbed her fingers over the smooth surface, admiring the colors. The temptation was too great. She put one egg in one front pocket of the sweater and one egg in the other pocket. *No one will ever miss two eggs,* she thought, as she turned to leave.

As she emerged from the henhouse, the sunlight blinded her and she tripped over the threshold. The next thing she knew, she was flat on her face in the dirt.

Jumping up, she brushed her sleeves and the bottom of her dress. Wet egg slime covered the palms of her hands. Egg yolks dripped through the pockets of her pink sweater. "My sweater!" she gasped. "Oh no! My beautiful pink sweater!"

Carefully, she slipped it off, trying not to get egg goo on her skin. She then wiped her hands with the clean part of the sweater and bundled it up. *I can't tell Mother I stole two eggs, but how do I explain the eggs on the sweater? I'm going to get in trouble . . . again.*

When Roxane arrived home, she sneaked in through the front door instead of going through the kitchen. Hittie heard her and called out, "How did the girls like it?"

"They loved it," Roxane replied as she grabbed the thick, wooden banister and propelled herself up the stairs. Her stomach was in knots and her eyes blurred with tears. She wanted to clean the sweater but would be late to work. She stuffed it into the bottom of the armoire, changed her dress, then trudged to her house cleaning job to earn the last fifty cents.

That night was weekly bath night. In the morning Roxane had helped Oliver bring up the galvanized tub from down cellar to put on the back of the kitchen stove. Then they had taken turns carrying big dippers of water from the pump to fill it. It took the whole day for the water to heat up. After supper, they pulled two heavy kitchen chairs in front of the open oven door, making sure the seats faced each other. A washtub was set onto the chairs and filled with regular water along with the hot water. Each week, Oliver and Roxane switched who went first. That night Oliver bathed first.[19]

When Roxane had her turn and eased down into the now tepid water, she thought she would feel better. Baths always made her feel better. But she felt bad about taking the eggs and not telling her mother the truth. The queasy feeling in her stomach wouldn't go away.

⁓

Sunday morning, as the family assembled in the kitchen for the short walk to church, Hittie looked over at Roxane who was wearing a plain cotton dress and her navy blue cardigan. "Roxane, dear. All you've been talking about for weeks is that pink sweater. You can wear it on Sundays, you know."

Buttoning the cardigan, Roxane coolly replied, "I think I'll save the pink sweater for *very special days*," and continued out the front door, hoping her problems would go away if she kept the sweater hidden.

After church, Roxane decided to clean the sweater. When she opened the armoire, a smell like a mixture of vinegar, vomit, and sulfur blasted into her face. Quickly closing and latching the door, she ran downstairs to get a rag. After rubbing the rag with soap and water, she went back up to blot the weepy, egg-soaked fabric.

Taking a deep breath, she opened the armoire, knelt on the floor, and wiped the sweater with three strokes, then exhaled and slammed the door. Once again, she took a deep breath, opened it up, wiped the sweater, then shut it. There was still egg mess on it. She frowned, wondering what to do next. But first, breathing through her mouth, she rushed across the room and threw open the window for a bit of air.

Now she had to get rid of the rag without being seen. Behind the barn was the burn pile where her dad burned household trash every so often. Roxane hid the rag under other trash, then returned to the house.

⌒

After school on Monday, her mother met her at the kitchen door.

Roxane knew this was going to be *the moment* and braced herself.

"Roxane, dear. There are bags of wool scraps and a couple of blankets I want to put in mothballs—like the blue blanket in your room. Would you run down to the store and buy me a box?"

Thinking quickly, Roxane responded, "I'll stay here and help you." Roxane didn't want her mother going into her room. "Oliver can go to the store. I'll collect what you need *from our rooms* so you can pack them in the chest."

Hittie headed inside. "Good idea. That's so kind of you."

Roxane let out a deep breath. *That was close. How am I going to keep my mother out of my room?*

That night at supper, Roxane made a request. It was a fib, actually. "I'm starting to make a surprise for baby Desmond."

Oliver raised his eyebrows as he looked over at her.

"Please don't go in my room this week. I'm keeping it a secret. I don't want you to see what I'm doing. I'm keeping the door closed." Her dad was at the Chatham Life-Saving Station, but her mother and brother agreed to stay away from her room.

When Hittie left the table to go to the kitchen, Oliver leaned over and whispered, "What are you making for Des?"

"A bib."

"You can sew?" he asked and then chuckled.

Roxane grimaced. *Another lie! I can't sew a stitch and he knows it.*

⌒

When Roxane arrived home from school on Tuesday, her mother met her at the back door. "Roxane, dear. I know you want to work on the surprise for Desmond. Instead of helping me in the kitchen, why don't you spend the rest of the afternoon in your room? I'll just be making up a fruit breakfast cake anyway."

Roxane's eyes grew wide. *No! I don't want to be in that stinky room!* "All right, Mother," she responded calmly, entering the kitchen. She then proceeded to flop up the stairs as if accepting punishment. She met Oliver coming down.

"Something wrong?" he asked. "What *did* you do this time?"

She stomped past Oliver, closed and latched her bedroom door, and collapsed on the bed. Grabbing a pillow, she pulled it over her face to block out the egg smell. She didn't want to be in her bedroom all afternoon. "I want to be outside!" she whined. After a while, she decided to sit on the floor and just dig her eyes into a book.

That night after supper, Roxane crept into the pantry and found cinnamon and nutmeg next to the molasses. The foul, rancid odor of rotting eggs in her room was unbearable and this was a last-ditch effort. After wrapping the spices securely in a hankie, she slipped the bundle into her pocket, sauntered through the kitchen as if nothing was going on, then hot-tailed it up the stairs to her bedroom.

Suddenly, the floor creaked and a knock sounded at her bedroom door. She froze. "Who is it?"

"Oliver. When you want to talk, let me know." He left.

When she was ready for bed, she set the spices on the pillow right next to her nose. She acknowledged that she had to make up new lies to cover the old lies and it was getting more difficult to remember which lies were told when or to whom, but at least that night she was able to fall asleep without dreaming of being covered in vomit or enduring a hundred lashes.

A week later

Roxane skipped up the steps, just back from school.

Her mother met her at the door with Desmond in her arms. "Today I went into your bedroom to get one of your dresses," she divulged, "and the odor of rotten eggs nearly finished me off! The sweater is ruined."[20]

Roxane was so choked up she couldn't speak.

"Come on," her mother ordered with teeth clenched. "Walk with me to the barn and back. You have some explaining to do. So, you wanted to save the sweater for *very special days*? Hah."

Roxane then told her mother the whole story. "Can you wash the sweater?" she asked.

"No. The smell is so bad it will never come out."

It seemed her mother was rather understanding about all of this, but she wasn't fooled. Dad would give her a spanking the next time he was home from the life-saving station and that would be the second time this month.

Hittie stopped at the barn. "I assume you're not making a surprise for Desmond."

"Well, no," admitted Roxane, "but I drew a woodpecker on a quahog shell and can give that to him."

Hittie turned around and started for the house, thoroughly disgusted.

Roxane flopped on the grass. Tippy trotted over. She folded her arms around his neck, nearly choking him senseless and kissed him on the nose. "I love that sweater and felt so pretty in it. And special."

Tippy wagged his tail, slid to the grass, and rested his chin on her legs.

"You love me, don't you boy?" She stroked his head and scratched his cheeks.

Tippy lifted his head to gaze at her.

"Yes, I love you too. Do you like me in pink?" She paused, taking in the dog's comment. "I do, too."

Oliver came from the barn and sat beside Roxane. "I heard what was going on."

She looked over at Oliver and thought about how he innately feels the currents and tides when out fishing and how he does chores every day without complaint. He was just so *good*. "Do you think telling the truth right at the start would have saved the sweater?"

Oliver leaned back with his elbows on the grass. "Maybe." They sat in silence. "But perhaps not." He stretched out on the ground. "Mother always says, 'everything happens for a reason.'"

Roxane's chin went up. "I'm not going to let one stupid thing get me down." She stood and started towards the house.

Something caught her eye.

She looked over her shoulder at the burn pile out back of the barn. There, on top of the heap, was a scrunched up wad of pink fluff.

THE END

Conversation

1) Skipper was proud of Roxane for earning money for the sweater saying, "You accomplish what you set out to do. That's what's important." Share a time you set out to do something difficult or unusual and succeeded.

2) Proverbs 16:18 states that "Pride goeth before a fall." How does that verse relate to this story?

3) In the early 1900s, many townspeople didn't lock doors to their homes nor fence their yards. Children played outside and roamed freely. Today, children are not only constantly supervised, but parents take on the responsibility of entertaining them. Share reasons why these lifestyles are so different. Is there a way to balance some of the old ways with today?

Doing

<u>Research</u>: Roxane's great-grandfather, Captain Oliver Eldredge (b.1810), acquired the town gristmill after the Civil War. The milled grain had a short shelf life so it had to be used quickly. That's why women would spend one day each week baking bread, biscuits, and cake. Around 1910, white flour, with its longer shelf life, became available. Baking could now be done at any time. Compare the nutritional content of flours used today.

Hittie's Fish Chowder:

1) Start with a firm, whole white fish like haddock or cod. Fillet the fish and cut into 2-inch pieces. Set aside.

2) In a deep pot, add the fish carcass, 6 cups of cold water, some onion and celery pieces, bay leaves, thyme and any other spices or herbs you may like. Bring to a boil and simmer for 30 minutes. Strain. Return the broth to the pot and continue to simmer to reduce down.

3) In another pot, cook chopped bacon along with diced onion. Add cut potatoes and 2 cups of hot water. Cook until potatoes are tender. Add potato mixture and the fish pieces to the simmering fish stock and simmer an additional 10 minutes. Add 1 cup half & half. Season with butter, salt and pepper. Reheat and serve.

Sprayed

November, 1913 – Roxane, age 9
Chatham, Cape Cod, Massachusetts

"Stay out!"

Miss Bassett's shrill voice resounded in the crowded one-room schoolhouse as she marched over to Oliver and Roxane, who had just arrived. Silence filled the room as all the children turned to stare. "Sit in the entry until you air out." She waited. "Your coats?"

Oliver and Roxane took off their coats and handed them to their teacher.

Miss Bassett opened a window and hung the coats outside on a hook, then closed and latched it. She pointed. "Three hours in the entry. I'll bring you work when I can."

Roxane, still rather pale and queasy, sank to the floor of the school entry and pushed back against the wall. Shivering, she pulled her dress tight around her ankles and crossed her arms against the damp cold. Her gaze followed her older brother Oliver as he seated himself on a cranberry crate.

Their eyes met. Laughter bubbled over as last night's adventure replayed in her mind.

The previous night

"Hurry up, Roxane," Oliver hollered, as he looked up the stairs and pulled on his coat. "The moon is full so we will easily find the traps." He strode across the hardwood floor and onto the large, braided rug in the front room.[21] "Dad, Roxane and I will check the traps. Back in an hour or so."

"Fine, fine," mumbled Skipper Eldredge as he updated the income register at the roll-top desk. He had taught Oliver to take care of farm animals, man a small boat, dig for oysters and clams, and hunt. Even though Oliver was only eleven, Skipper trusted his ability and judgment. "Give me a shout if you get more than two. We'll need to skin 'em tonight."

Upstairs, Roxane quickly donned a cardigan. "I'll be right there! I want to come!" she yelled. "Wait for me!" The tall nine-year-old hurried down the stairs and through the kitchen to collect her coat, but Oliver was already out the kitchen door. Deciding to wait just inside the door, she tied on her knitted hat so she would be ready when he returned from the barn with the equipment.

While peering out the window into the moonlit night, shadows dancing over the ground, the image of a skunk came to mind. She smiled.

On Halloween, just a fortnight ago, she and Oliver played a prank for a bit of fun. They had found an old, black stocking with holes in it. After stuffing it full of white rags, Oliver tied a long piece of string around it so he could pull it and make it look something like a skunk. Later that night, after dark, they put the make-believe skunk on the sidewalk in front of Wiskie Taylor's house.

"Roxane, hold the skunk here. I'll stretch the string across the street," Oliver whispered, his eyes having adjusted to the black of night. When the string was set behind Cyrus Kent's fence, Roxane hurried across the street to where Oliver was kneeling.

In a few minutes, a couple approached, walking down the middle of the street. Oliver pulled the string. The woman's scream shattered the night.

"Skunk!" the man yelled as he grabbed his wife's arm. "Come on!"

Roxane and Oliver looked at each other and giggled. Sneaking out from their hiding spot, Roxane went back across the street to set up the stocking-skunk again, her eyes full of mischief.

A few minutes later, Pa Perry came by on his bicycle.

Oliver pulled the string a bit too tightly. The string got caught in the bicycle pedals. "Doggonit!" Oliver spit out. He and Roxane ran after the bicycle as it dragged their "skunk" nearly to Main Street.[22]

The Halloween escapade banished from her thoughts as light from Oliver's lantern bobbed along the cart track from the barn. *Tonight is not a night for playing. This night is for bringing in money.* She stepped out the back door into the fresh night air to join Oliver.

"Take this empty sack," he said, as he shifted a pack of gear on his shoulder. "Just watch what I do. You'll learn."

At a brisk pace, they made their way toward the shore where skunks slept in dens along the marshes. "Skunks aren't true winter hibernators," Oliver explained. "They come out of their dens to eat small animals and sometimes beach grass—which no other critter will eat."

"Will you trap into February this year?" Roxane asked. "I heard Mr. Gould say you can hunt skunk in any month with an *R* in it."

Oliver kept walking, intent on his mission. "We need to keep the traps set through January. We'll get some muskrat too." As if making it clear, he added, "Skunks mate in February."

As they approached the first trap, Roxane spoke in a whisper. "Look at that!"

Oliver set the sack of gear down and extracted the club and rabbit meat bait. He didn't need the club to break the back of this skunk. The deadfall trap had killed it. "Sack," he ordered, over his shoulder.

Roxane tip-toed to Oliver and held open the empty bag.

Oliver gently lowered the dead animal into it, careful not to rupture any glands. There was a bit of odor, but he was used to it. He then re-set the trap with bait, gathered his gear, picked up the sack, and moved on to check the next trap.

Within an hour they had collected three skunks. One was pure black and would fetch a price of three dollars, which was fifty cents more than a skunk with a white stripe. There were already five glossy skunk pelts pinned to the wall back at the barn, having been washed, tanned, and oiled. Roxane knew her brother could skin with no cuts on the hide and she vowed to learn how to do that, too.

Roxane lifted the sack of dead skunks to judge the weight. "Let me carry the sack. It's not too heavy. I can do it." She wanted to be a real help instead of just tagging along.

Oliver studied her determined expression. "All right," he decided, "but be careful."

After ten minutes, twenty or more pounds of skunk got a bit heavy, so she switched the sack to her other shoulder. Misjudging the weight, the sack swung wildly, causing her to lose her balance. She stumbled. The sack fell to the ground with a thud.

Roxane crumpled to her knees, gasping for breath. An unnatural sound ripped from her throat.

Oliver turned. "Doggonit!" The rank, putrid, stench of skunk spray was overpowering at point blank. He inhaled into the arm of his coat.

Within seconds Roxane was throwing up. Vomit oozed from her nose. Heaving and sputtering, she attempted to speak. "I didn't know skunks can . . . can spray," she wheezed, "even when they're dead."

"Now you know." Oliver's pained expression was evident as he reluctantly picked up the sack and reached for Roxane. "Let's get home."

Roxane had a sudden realization. "Dad!" she faltered.

"What will Dad say . . . when . . . when we get home?" She promptly stopped and retched again.

Oliver was always prosaic. "He already smells we got skunk."

Back at school

In the entry at school, Roxane stopped laughing. She still didn't feel too good. "It's not fair," she complained, as she twirled her hair with her right fingers. "The smell doesn't bother you."

"Actually, it does." Oliver didn't mention he had thrown up last night too. "Even now, it's bothering the whole school and probably the whole town. Fresh air will do us good. Let's go outside." He opened the front door and stepped out into the brisk air.

Roxane descended the six steps, then started searching for a particular kind of rock.

Oliver leaned against the side of the school building and yawned. "We have what, a half hour of just waiting here? What are you doing?"

"I'm looking for a rock to write with. I'm mad at Effie for running in the opposite direction when she saw me this morning. She's my best friend." Now on her knees, Roxane started to scrape on one of the slate steps that led to the school. "I suppose the smell will never get out of my coat. Will it be thrown on the burn pile?"

Oliver thought for a moment. "No. Hang your coat on the backside of the barn. Wear it when you go hunting with me."

Roxane looked up with wide eyes.

"You're my partner now. This won't be the last time we get sprayed. Wear one of my heavy shirts over your dress until Mother finds you another coat." Oliver walked over to where she was writing. "*Mephitis mephitis*. What does that mean?"

"You don't know?" Roxane smiled up at her brother. "You mean I know something you don't know? It's the Latin name for skunk. It means, *double foul odor*. That's us."

Oliver laughed.

THE END

Conversation

1) What remedies are used today to get rid of skunk odor in clothing?

2) Recently, the one-room schoolhouse model has gained in popularity. What are the advantages of this model in terms of peer-based or team-based learning?

3) Look on the internet for "Rules for Teachers in 1915." Discuss the twelve rules and why they were put in place. What behavioral expectations are required of teachers outside of school today?

4) In addition to school, Roxane was expected to complete indoor and outdoor chores and earn money for the family. What were you expected to do as a child to help your family?

Doing

Research: Compare a man's daily wage in 1910 with a $2.50 skunk pelt.

Research: What were skunk pelts used for?

Tracks:

    a. Try to identify a few animal tracks while out hiking.

    b. For a mural project in one room of the house, paint different animal tracks in various colors going in a window and out the door, or in one window and out another window.

Electricity: In 1916, three years after this story, none of the 568 homes in the town of Chatham had electricity—or running water. To generate an appreciation for electrical lighting and for a bit of fun, designate a day like Candlemas Day on February 2 to go without electric lights in your home. Only use candles, lanterns, and flashlights.

1 Roxane's father, Surfman Ernest "Skipper" Eldredge, in his U.S. Life-Saving Service uniform. (Photo 1900)

2 Eldredge Family: Oliver, Mehitable "Hittie," Ernest "Skipper," Roxane (Photo c. 1908)

3 Located at 85 Cross Street in Chatham, Massachusetts, this house was built by Skipper in 1904 while he was on summer leave from the U.S. Life-Saving Service. (Photo early 1900s)

4 Doll furniture Skipper made for Roxane out of cranberry crates. Size: large chest 14x9x20, small chest 11x7x13, bed 19x12x11. The fur neck-warmer draped on the chest is hand-made from the early 1900s. "Saturday Treat"

5 Roxane (Photo c. 1909)

6 Built in 1797 by Benjamin Godfrey, the gristmill on Mill Hill had been owned by Roxane's great-grandfather, Captain Oliver Eldredge (b.1810) from 1865-1883. (Photo 1900)

7 Skipper and his brother Ralph regularly walked by the mill on their way to and from work. They also grew up nearby. "Saturday Treat" (Photo 1894)

8 Roxane Eldredge's maternal grandparents, Captain Stephen and Caroline Gould lived in this home on the hill above the shanties on Oyster River in West Chatham, Massachusetts. Roxane was born here on September 22, 1904. In October, her family moved into their new home at 85 Cross Street. "The Cold Fire"

9 Oyster River: Captain Stephen Gould started S. W. Gould & Son Shellfish Merchants here in 1873. Skipper's shanty is to the right, where he worked from 1913 to 1963. (Photo c. 1940s) "The Cold Fire" "The Pianist"

10 Coming from Johnny Howes' dry goods store [Boston Store], Roxane paused here near Oyster Pond to pick dandelion greens before continuing toward home (right). (Photo 1910) "My Beautiful Pink Sweater"

11 Partial view of the large barn Skipper built that was used for their horse, cow, hay, tack, and cart. (Photo c. 1960) "My Beautiful Pink Sweater" "The Pianist"

12 Oliver, Roxane, and friend at the Howes brothers estate in Chatham. (Photo 1912) "My Beautiful Pink Sweater"

13 Atwood School (right) on Stage Harbor Road. Roxane and Oliver took the right fork here when walking to Oyster River in "The Cold Fire." They also attended this school. (Photo early 1900s) "Sprayed"

14 Desmond and Roxane (Photo c. 1914)

15 Having attained the age of 12, Oliver wears trousers and a jacket rather than knickers. (Photo 1915)

16 Looking east on Main Street, a blimp comes into view from the Chatham Naval Air Station during World War I. (Photo 1918) "The Pianist"

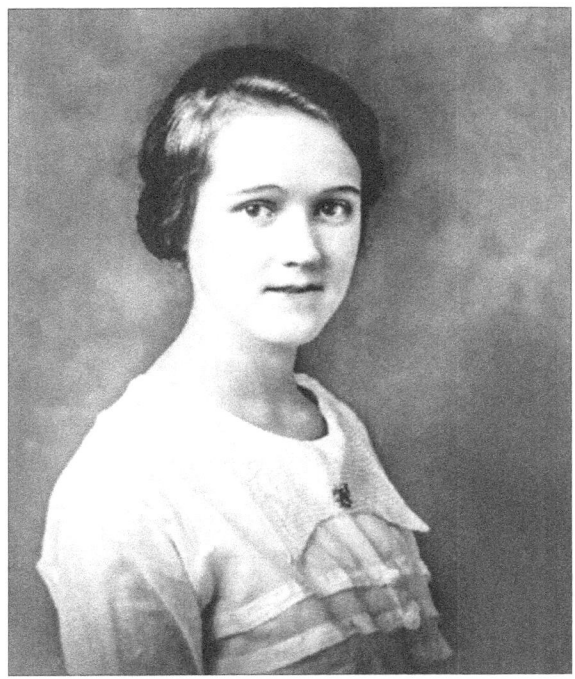

17 Roxane in high school. (Photo c. 1920)

18 Roxane (far left) writes at the top, "1922 Graduating class of Chatham High School on our Washington trip." (Photo 1922) "Finish Line"

19 Roxane fished here at Town Cove when she and her husband moved to Orleans. In this photo, men have dug a trench and are landing the transatlantic telegraph cable. The cable ship is moored out in deep water. (Photo 1891) "Out Fishing"

20 As an elementary school teacher from 1924–1929, Roxane was required to make sure students had cleaned the dirt from under their fingernails before entering the classroom. (Photo c. 1924)

The Pianist

Spring, 1919 ~ Roxane, age 14
Chatham, Cape Cod, Massachusetts

With a hot cup of tea warming her hands, Hittie relaxed onto a kitchen chair as Desmond, now six, appeared from nowhere, grabbed a few molasses cookies from the plate on the table and skittered away. She looked over at Roxane and continued their conversation. "We've had that piano since you were born. Yes, you've learned to play it and I'm proud of you. But now that you're fourteen, you don't play it much anymore."

"I have a lot of studying to do," Roxane countered. She twisted her hair into a ponytail and then let it flop. "I do practice sometimes to play for the Navy boys."

"I know dear, but maybe you can practice up at church. Our piano takes up half the front room. Wouldn't it be nice to have a couple of chairs in there for guests instead?" Hittie had thought long and hard the past year about selling the *square* piano. It was a massive, rectangular piece of furniture: seven feet long, over three feet in depth, and weighing over 700 pounds. "It's ornate and beautiful, but do we really need it? I think it's time to sell it." Hittie knew that selling the instrument would bring them needed money following the Great War.

"But we've always had the piano. It's part of the house. I love playing it. And it has such a soft sound, it doesn't bother anyone."

Hittie sighed, pushed up from the table, and lifted the

tea kettle from the stove. "True. But remember dear, nothing stays the same."

Roxane left the kitchen and started up the stairs to her bedroom. Her piano-playing days were numbered. She just didn't know it yet.

Sunday afternoon

Concentrating as she moved her hands over the keys, Roxane wanted the end of the piece filled with emotion. As the final phrase rose and fell, she slowed, paused on the second to the last chord, and lightly placed her hands for the final notes. Silence. The whole feeling was of something finished. Complete. This was the kind of music she liked to create. Notes on the page became sounds and those sounds led to a story that went on in her mind. That story richly complemented the composer's intentions.

Gathering the hymnbook and two other pieces of sheet music, she headed to the kitchen. At the open cellar door, she called out. "Mother, I'm leaving now." Then she shrugged into her sweater and coat from the hook near the back door.

Hittie emerged from down cellar with two jars of fruit for cobbler and carefully latched the door. "Before you go, a word. I know you're safe with Reverend and Mrs. Hyde but do be careful with all those sailors around. And remember to ask the Reverend what hymns are for next week. We'll be leaving Thursday on our shopping trip, so you'll have to get in your practicing." She set the jars on the counter. "We'll wait 'till you get home before we eat supper."

As Roxane strolled down the sandy road toward town, she took in the grass growing on the sides of the street and the white, picket fences defending the Cape half-houses. It seemed that just overnight, the leaves had fully opened. Turning left onto Main Street, she passed the town pump, the obelisk war monument dedicated to those who died in the Rebellion of 1861–1865, and continued to the Congregational Church with its white steeple.

As she neared the church, she glanced up. Lightning had struck the steeple many years before. A few men had repaired the top of the spire using part of the mast of a wrecked ship. *It's a landmark for ships at sea as well as for townspeople. It's a landmark for me . . . just like my piano.* Walking around the side of the church, she called out. "Hello!"

Reverend Hyde smiled and waved as he approached his borrowed automobile.[23] "Hello again, Roxane. You have gumption to attend the morning church service and then come back for another one."

Roxane liked the young Reverend Hyde and his wife. His rousing sermons and enthusiasm inspired the congregation. Never tiring, he reached out to the servicemen stationed at the Chatham Naval Air Station with a Sunday afternoon service. She was proud to be asked to go along.

"Are you ready to play?" Mrs. Hyde asked.

"I'm ready, but I know about the Saturday night parties. They bang the daylights out of the piano there and I never know which keys are playable."[24]

Mrs. Hyde opened the passenger door and slid in next to her husband, setting her prized violin between her legs. "That does make it difficult, especially when a key goes down and then doesn't come back up. Go ahead Roxane," she motioned, "jump in back. But you manage well. We're a great musical duo."

The car crawled along sandy roads and eventually across an expanse of moorland jutting out into Pleasant Bay. Rising from the beach grass were hangars for pontoon-type seaplanes and double hangars which housed large Curtiss HS flying boats. Roxane peered out the windows as they neared the base, hoping to spot the blimp. She couldn't decide if it looked more like a bloated fish or a fat cucumber.

After being admitted through the main cattle-guard

gate, they drove by the six-sided radio shack and the huge two-story barracks that housed 300 sailors. When they arrived at the Young Men's Christian Association (YMCA) hut, most of the sailors, even a few recovering from injuries, were already inside waiting for the church service to begin. A few stragglers were heading toward the building in their Sunday whites.

The YMCA not only held church services, but distributed athletic equipment, had areas for boxing matches, dances, and shows, and included a library. Most importantly, it operated the base cafeteria, known as the *canteen*. This was the hub.

"Hey, sweetheart!" One of the Navy boys winked at Roxane as she entered the building. "Come over and sit with us."

Roxane smiled a bit, then turned, aware of their stares as she followed Mrs. Hyde over to the piano corner. Reverend Hyde immediately greeted the men, engaging them in his friendly way.

Roxane set her music on the rack. "We'll do their favorite songs, right? *Throw out the Lifeline* and *Brightly Beams Our Father's Mercy?*"

"Yes," responded Mrs. Hyde as she set up her music stand, "we'll start with those."

The service began and the men sang with gusto.

> *Throw out the lifeline! Throw out the lifeline!*
> *Someone is drifting away.*
> *Throw out the lifeline! Throw out the lifeline!*
> *Someone is sinking today.*

Toward the end of the service, as Roxane and Mrs. Hyde were playing the final hymn, a string broke on Mrs. Hyde's violin and they were forced to stop.

A sailor (who was shell-shocked) yelled from the back in

a rather nasty tone, "If you can't do better than that, we will sing without the music!"

While Mrs. Hyde frantically tried to fix her violin, Roxane stood, and facing the sailors, simply replied, "We'll try to do better."

After the service, a sailor came over to the piano. "Hello Roxane. I'm Ben. Don't worry about the last hymn. I play cello and a broken string can happen to anyone. We like it when the Reverend brings you and Mrs. Hyde here. You cheer up the place." With a parting nod, he turned and joined the others for their typical Sunday supper: cold sliced meats, potato salad, cold beans with French dressing, bread with butter and jam, and tea.

Roxane's stomach growled as she slid into her coat and gathered her music. She knew her friends envied her for being around the handsome Navy boys. Perhaps she'd talk with cello-playing Ben next week. Maybe she could even talk Reverend and Mrs. Hyde into staying for supper. It was certainly worth all the piano practice to be the center of attention.

Four days later on Thursday morning

Skipper leaned against the kitchen counter, sipping coffee. Although they now had an electric pull-chain light in the ceiling, he preferred the soft lantern light in the pre-dawn darkness. Years of beach duty with the U.S. Life-Saving Service, particularly the shift beginning at four in the morning, made getting up early easy for him. But now in his fifth year as a shell-fisherman working alongside his wife's family at S. W. Gould & Son Shellfish Merchants, he was simply up early for the great Hittie-Roxane send-off.

Roxane bounded into the kitchen. "Dad, this is so much fun," she whispered. "Mother knows exactly which textile mills to go to. New Bedford Dry Goods expanded up, you know." Entering the cold pantry through a door with glass panes, she brought out their lunches and snacks, lightly kicking the pantry door closed behind her.

Skipper watched as Roxane flitted about the kitchen.

"It's so crowded there," Roxane continued, excitedly. "You wouldn't believe it. Mother asks me what yard goods I like, but there are so many to choose from, I can't decide. Mother knows exactly what to get." Roxane artfully arranged the food in a cloth bag. "Last fall, she told me she wanted to get all the sewing done by February but with the Spanish flu and not being able to travel, she frets because it's now April." She pulled on her coat and picked up her pocketbook and food bag stuffed with three extra-large bags then turned to her dad. "Don't ask. I've already practiced for the Navy boys' service and know the hymns."

Hittie swept into the kitchen, clutching a small blue suitcase stitched in white. Noting Roxane was ready, she bundled into her coat.

Skipper set down his coffee, trying to get used to the idea that Roxane was once again taking his place on this yearly three-day trip. "You're going to catch the noon boat from New Bedford to Woods Hole on Saturday?"

Hittie adjusted her hat. "We'll take that boat, then the train. I know the way, Skip. We'll get home." She glanced around to make sure all was in order. "Desmond is still asleep. Lunch and supper fixings are in the pantry." While hugging him she spoke softly about the Spanish flu. "If the train is packed to the gills," she assured him, "we have scarves we can wrap around our faces. The worst of the grippe has passed." She smiled into his eyes. "We are off. Bye!"

Skipper held the kitchen door open for them and watched as they started at a brisk pace down the sandy drive. Just a smidgen of light came from the overcast sky in the damp and chilly early morning hour. As he reentered the kitchen, his mind churned at the possibilities that lay before him while his womenfolk were away.

Two days later on Saturday evening

Hittie and Roxane, both weary from their long day of travel, pushed open the back door. "Hello, we're home," Hittie called out, happy to be back in the warmth of her kitchen. "The weatherman was good to us."

Desmond rushed over to see the packages they dumped on the dining room table. Skipper rose from the rocking chair in the front room.

"My legs are so tired, I can't walk another step," uttered Roxane. "My shoulder hurts from carrying all this." She smiled brightly. "Dad, look at all the yard goods." She opened a package. "Mother found some flannel you'll really like. Look at this." She smoothed the checkered black and red flannel. "Don't you love it? We have material for you too, Des."

Desmond pointed to the parlor, exploding with news. "The piano . . . is . . . gone."

Roxane turned and stared. "What?"

Hittie's eyes grew wide. "You sold the piano?" She rushed into the room, then turned back to Skipper. "Well, that's good. I didn't know anyone who wanted it."

"You didn't want it. You've complained about it for a year. It's out of here. On the woodpile." Skipper stood still, knowing his was the last word. From his ship captain family and his work as a surfman, there was one person in command. In his home, he was that person.

Shocked, Roxane stared at her dad. "It's on the woodpile?" She then respectfully zipped her lips.

Desmond grabbed Roxane's hand and started pulling her. "Come on. I'll show you."

"That's all right, Des. I'll go by myself." She stooped

down to his level. "You stay here. We'll look at it together tomorrow." Roxane shrugged back into her coat, put on her hat, and lit a lantern. *I knew they were going to take away the piano, but I didn't know it would happen so soon.*

With deliberate steps, she followed the ruts of the cart track around to the side of the barn. Lifting the light high, reality hit her. Her dear piano. Stacked kindling. Turning, she found her way into the barn.

Setting the lantern on the floor, she settled against the wall with her knees hunched up to her chin.

Oliver, people will think I'm crazy if they ever find out I come here to talk to you. Why aren't you right over there, brushing down the mare? Roxane's brother Oliver had died suddenly of a ruptured appendix three years earlier.[25] She missed him dreadfully. *My piano's gone. Dad doesn't care. Mother doesn't understand. The piano was my friend. It's like something's been ripped from my chest. Playing the piano is like having a relationship—not with a person, but with sound. You understand, right?*

She dabbed at the tears welling in her eyes. *It's not easy to get to church to practice and the piano there is pretty bad. My days as a pianist are over, aren't they? I will never play again for the Navy boys or for my friends to sing Christmas carols. What would you say, brother? Face it? Move on? There's a reason for everything? Forgive and forget? I'm so sad, Oliver. I don't want things to change.*

Taking up the lantern, Roxane made her way back to the woodpile to look for some ivory keys. *I'll take a few to put in my jewelry box.* After poking through a pile of wood scraps, she gave up, not finding even one.

With nothing left to do, she extinguished the lantern and started toward the house. In the dark, the kitchen light blazed through the window like it was calling to her. Yet she felt defeated. Alone. Tippy wasn't even there to trot alongside her. His burial place was out back. He'd been her devoted pal. Even-tempered. Eager to please. He had been a true friend. His was pure love.

Hittie met her at the door and gave her a hug. "Ah Roxane, dear. It's not my place to say anything, but we should have sold the piano. We need the money. I had no idea Dad would chop it up." To herself she added . . . *and the next time he even thinks of doing something idiotic, he should run it by me first.*

Taking down a couple of soup bowls, she tried to make the best of it. "No matter. What's done is done. You can't go back. Just forward." She turned and leaned against the counter. "You know? You could turn to the art of cooking. That's surely a more necessary skill than piano playing. I'll roast a hen for Sunday dinner tomorrow and then we can ...."

Gliding through the kitchen with a heavy heart, Roxane nodded to her mother and then ascended the stairs as her mother's voice faded away.

Epilogue

Later in life, Roxane commented, "We never found out what happened to the ivory keys." She continued with the story, chuckling as she related it:

> "One afternoon, Dad fell asleep in the platform rocker and fell over to the right side. His arms were very long, so his right hand was near the rocker. The phone rang and startled him. He came forward and crushed the fingers on his right hand. In an hour, that platform rocker was out on the woodpile with the piano. Dad loved to chop wood. We had some expensive kindling wood."[26]

THE END

Conversation

1) Imagine what it was like for Hittie to go on a once-a-year shopping trip to buy material to make clothes for her family. Describe the planning involved if you could only shop for clothes once a year.

2) Skipper, a carpenter by trade, built and sold fine furniture and knew the value of workmanship. Why did he chop up the hand-carved piano instead of selling it? How do you decide whether to throw away material items, donate them, or sell them?

3) Why does Roxane gravitate to the barn and casually talk to Oliver's spirit? How does the loss of her piano connect with the death of her brother and even the family dog?

4) Comment on Hittie Eldredge's remarks: "Nothing stays the same," and "You can't go back. Just forward." Discuss the poem "Old Maps No Longer Work" by Joyce Rupp.

5) Roxane once stated, "Mother hoped her children might become musicians, but we failed her."[27] (Actually, Roxane was a highly-accomplished pianist at the time of this story.) Did your parents have expectations for you or your siblings that never materialized? Discuss.

Doing

<u>Research</u>: The Chatham Naval Air Station, built in 1917 as a base for anti-submarine patrols, used Curtiss R-9s, Curtiss HS-1L, 2L flying boats, and blimps. The planes,

flying at 1,000 feet, kept track of ships in the area, often circling around them for hours looking for the threat of U-boats.

  a. For reconnaissance, one plane headed north, while the other went south. Radio communication between the planes and the Chatham station was unreliable, so pigeons were used to carry messages back to the base. Each plane carried two birds. The birds in the northbound plane were trained to fly south to the base and those in the southbound plane were trained to fly north. Interestingly, the birds could fly only in daylight on days with no fog—and fog is common in the Chatham area. Look into the use of carrier pigeons during World War I.

  b. What was the Chatham Naval Air Station response to the German attack off Orleans, Massachusetts on July 21, 1918?

Research: In her journal, Roxane spoke of a Navy man who reacted to the violin string breaking by yelling out, "If you can't do better than that, we will sing without the music!" Apparently, people knew he was shell shocked. What does the World War I era term "shell shock" mean? Why were some shell-shocked soldiers executed? Compare the differences between shell shock and post-traumatic stress disorder (PTSD).

Songs: Sing popular songs of the time: "Take Me Out to the Ballgame" or "You're a Grand Old Flag."

Grandma's Cobbler:

1) Use 4 to 6 cups of ripe, juicy summer fruits, such as peaches, blueberries, or blackberries. Cut the fruit if needed and add to a saucepan with a bit of sugar and perhaps a tad of water. Heat the fruit mixture until hot and keep warm until needed. The heated fruit (the secret to a great cobbler) will help cook the biscuit dough.

2) In a bowl, combine 1 cup of flour, 1½ teaspoons baking powder, 2 teaspoons sugar, and 1/2 teaspoon salt. Pour in 1/4 cup oil and 2/3 cup milk and stir just until moistened.

3) Put the warm fruit into a square baking pan or pie pan. Spread spoonfuls of the batter over fruit. Sprinkle the top with sugar. Bake in a 350° F oven 15 minutes or until biscuit dough is done.

Note: Today, dry ingredients are combined and then wet ingredients are blended into the dry mixture. Back in the day however, wet ingredients were mixed first and then flour was added until it "felt right" since at the time, flour was not standardized.

Finish Line

June 20 and 28, 1922 ~ Roxane, age 17
Chatham, Cape Cod, Massachusetts

"Hello Uncle Ralph!" Roxane knocked on the front door and walked in. She always liked his house. Light spilled into the interior through the fine windows.

"Over here," Ralph called.

Roxane strode into the living room and dropped her bookbag on a chair. "I have news!"

Ralph, reclining in a chair with his feet propped on an old, round hassock, set down a stack of papers. "Let's see. I can't imagine. You were a tad worried you'd get B's on the final exams." Expecting she got A's but acting the part of the supportive uncle, he continued. "Don't feel bad, little one. You gave it your best effort. That's what counts."

"I didn't get B's." Standing straight and tall, she took a deep breath and made the announcement: "I'm valedictorian."

Ralph grinned. "Miss Valedictorian! My soul and body! Not only top of the class, but off to college. Quite an achievement, I'd say." He watched as she took a turn about the room looking concerned and wondered what she was up to. He liked her frank, matter-of-fact ways. Oh yes, she could sit with her hands folded like the other girls, but she was much more at home laughing as she hauled fish aboard a boat or talking political issues.

Roxane paused. "I have to write a speech for next Wednesday's graduation. I don't know what to say." She dove into her frustration. "I'm mad at my friends for teasing me on our class trip.[28] Remember we stayed at Hotel Driscoll? It's right across from the U.S. Capitol. We ate our meals there. They said I'm the same height as our server. That we were in love and should get married." She placed her hands on her hips. "Plus, they didn't like me leaving a three cent tip under my plate for him when they only gave a penny."

"Who was this server?"

"A colored man." She then whispered confidentially, "Most of us had never seen a colored person or an Oriental." She nodded, raising her eyebrows.

"I see." Needing a moment to gather his thoughts on that issue, he changed the subject. "Why don't you make tea? There's a cake on the shelf. I'll follow you in a couple of minutes."

Roxane was not to be diverted. She resumed her restless pacing. "Dad says when ships from other countries wrecked on our shore, he treated the sailors with dignity and respect, even though they couldn't speak English and weren't like us." In a tone of strong resolution, she continued. "I feel sorry for that server. People from different races can't marry, right? Can you imagine how horrified he must have been to hear the suggestion we marry?"

"What did your mother say?"

"You know Mother. She said, 'God bless them all.' I tell you, I have forgiven my friends. I just think my speech should include how to respect people of different nationalities and race. I just don't know where to begin!" On that grand valediction, she exited to the kitchen.

Ralph inhaled as deeply as he was able. The injury he had sustained from breathing poison gas on a World War I battlefield had so scarred his lungs, he had never regained full use of them. Now, simply standing from a seated position was difficult. Slowly, he made his way to the kitchen.

Roxane sliced the cake as she waited for water to boil.

Taking a seat in a rocking chair, Ralph began in his gentle way. "You know, little one, lecturing your classmates might not be the thing."

"Why?" she protested impulsively. "Someone needs to show them what's right."

He lounged in the chair, observing his niece with a bit of amusement. "Nothing is more tiresome than being told you're doing something wrong. From what you've disclosed, you spoke by your actions. I dare say they even wish they'd given a larger tip. Perhaps the lesson's been learned."

Roxane was silent, fixed on his words.

Ralph took a bite of cake, then continued while Roxane poured tea. "It's my belief that people fervently desire what is out of reach. Give them hope. Perhaps connect leaving high school with life at sea."

"You mean like the Eldredge family ship captains?"

Ralph pondered this as he held his warm teacup, then took several short breaths to get air into his lungs before he spoke. "Maybe not merchant ship captains but explorers."

Roxane hit the mark. "Explorers go to unknown lands just like we went to Washington D.C. and Philadelphia. We sailed from Fall River down Long Island Sound."

"Exactly," agreed Ralph, "but you need not mention your class trip." He set down the teacup, leaned back and crossed his arms. "The key to survival on board ship is preparation. Not that storms can't come at you."

Roxane looked rather struck by this. "We are off to explore. Discover." She then clapped her hands excitedly. "I knew you'd help me!" She then paused, remembering those were the exact words she'd said to Oliver so long ago when she had wanted a pink sweater. She pressed down the last crumbs of cake with her fork to clean her plate and took a sip of tea.

Ralph continued. "Keep in mind this here's a celebration."

"You're right," she said with purpose. "I need to get these ideas on paper. I've got to go." She glanced over at the sideboard. "You have that photo of me."

Ralph took a sip of tea. "And I'll wear it out just by looking at it!"

Roxane placed her teacup, plate, and fork neatly by the sink, then tucked her chair under the table. She turned to her uncle. "Would you listen to me practice the final version?"

Ralph smiled. "Of course, little one. I'd be honored." He always enjoyed calling her "little one" since she was tall like all the other Eldredges. It was he who was the runt of the family.

Roxane sparkled. "You're my favorite uncle, but don't tell anyone!" She then raced to the door, grabbing her bag on the way. "Bye!"

Ralph could not help but chuckle at that little quip she'd been saying since she was a child. A favored uncle is a good thing.

June 28, 8 p.m., Methodist-Episcopal Church, across from the Eldredge Library

Skipper stood at the outside of the pew waiting for the extended family to be seated before sliding in next to 9-year-old Desmond and Hittie. Everyone was dressed in their finest for the graduation ceremony. He looked at the ten students seated in the front row, knowing the original 9th grade class had started with twenty-two students. *So many drop out to work*, he thought, *just like I did when I was 14.* His mind flashed back to his time at sea with Captain Thomas Rogers on the fishing schooner *Flora Temple*. They followed schools of fish that took them to Block Island, Bar Harbor, and Halifax. *Yes*, he reflected, *a long time ago*.

Early in the ceremony, Mr. Charles Guild, the school principal, introduced Roxane. With practiced calm and an air of confidence, she ascended to the podium. Her valedictorian speech began with a story from literature and then in a clear, strong voice, she continued:

> "Like the explorer, who fits out his ships for the purpose of exploring unknown lands, we have been fitting out our ships and making other preparations for the purpose of exploring, what is to us, unknown lands. For twelve long years, we have been making preparations, surely a sufficiently long time, and longer than most explorers take. Just as the food supply and other necessities have been placed on board the ship, so the languages, history, and commercial subjects have been placed on board our ship, the mind. Of course, we have retained all that was ever stored there!"[29]

Skipper listened as she gave credit to teachers who instilled in her and her fellow students a spirit for citizenship, spoke of the meaning of success, and referred to their class motto: *He conquers who endures*. Roxane then concluded:

> "The ship having been made ready, we are about to set sail, and just as the explorer stands on the deck and waves a last good-bye, so we too bid farewell to the Chatham High."[30]

The Alumni Association immediately presented Roxane with a ten-dollar gold piece—the only award given that year. The audience stood, erupting into applause.

As they resumed their seats, Hittie placed her hand over Skipper's strong hand and leaned into him. "It's different now," she whispered, "like the world's off-kilter. Roxane leaving. Streetlights. Autos. Voting." She reached for her hankie, tucked in the cuff of her blouse.

Skipper gave her hand a gentle squeeze and smiled

reassuringly. He would greatly miss Roxane when she headed to college. A slight movement made him glance over his shoulder to the pew behind.

His brother Ralph broke into a smile and gave a nod. "Well done."[31]

THE END

Conversation

1) Most people who lived in small towns didn't travel unless it was necessary. Vacations, as we know them, were not a part of life. Thus, the seniors of Chatham High School were granted an amazing opportunity. They set off on April 14, 1922 for a week-long visit to Washington D.C. and Philadelphia. The most incredible thing for them was the zoo. They spoke of "monkeys, gorillas, an elephant, and a giraffe."[32] Share your recollections of the first time you travelled far from your hometown without your parents.

2) When thinking back on her schooling years, Roxane wrote, "What wonderful people there are in this world to give us a chance to make something of ourselves."[33] Name one or two people who have been supportive in your pursuits. Share how they influenced you.

3) Roxane, who was outspoken about political issues and admitted she always wanted to straighten out people's affairs, once prayed, "Teach me the glorious lesson that occasionally it is possible that I may be mistaken."[34] When is it time to stay silent about an issue or problem, and when is it time to speak out? Give examples.

4) At this time, when electricity used in homes, businesses, or churches was in its early stages, service was erratic. Lights could go out at any time. Thus, even at Roxane's graduation ceremony, candles and lanterns were on hand. Today, how are you prepared to cope for an extended time if electricity goes out in your area?

Doing

<u>Research</u>: Look into the history of restaurant tipping in America.

<u>Research</u>: Investigate miscegenation laws that prohibited interracial marriage.

<u>Napkin Folding</u>: Chatham High School students experienced formal dining on their class trip. Table settings included intricately folded napkins, which by the late 1800s had become an art form. With cloth napkins, learn to fold a zoo animal or flower.

Out Fishing

Dedicated to the French Cable Station Museum

October, 1929 – Roxane, age 25
Tonset Road Residence and Town Cove,
Orleans, Cape Cod, Massachusetts

"Roxane," Alaric called. "Are you here? Hello? Roxane...." Silence.

It had been a hot October day. Alaric was tired and glad to be home. As a lineman for the local utility, he and his crew had just spent the day repairing power lines. Although it was only just after four o'clock, he was starving. At age 23 with 225 pounds filling his six-foot, four-inch frame, he could put away a lot of food. His mouth watered at the thought of cod soaked in milk, then breaded and fried.

He set his metal lunch pail on the kitchen table and read the note lying there: *10 a.m. Out fishing. Love, R.* He looked around. Just that morning she had promised the best apple pie ever and four loaves of bread, yet there was no sign of baking.

Pushing open the screen door he yelled again. "Roxane, are you out here? Where are you?" Life was certainly a kick with Roxane. They'd been married in the living room of her childhood home in Chatham a month ago, followed by a Niagara Falls honeymoon. What a whirlwind to get settled in this house. *My home*, he thought. *My bride.*

He wandered past the fenced vegetable garden and around massive locust trees staking their claim in the woodlot. In the shed, the fishing pole and gear were gone. *She can't still be fishing.*

He took off at a run down the road, then followed a narrow path through densely packed bushes to Town Cove. Their rowboat was gone. Stooping forward to catch his breath, conscious of his heart thudding, he scanned the green marshes along the edge of the inlet, noting the few sailboats anchored a distance from shore. Not a soul was in sight.

Then he saw it. Right out in the middle of the cove with Roxane in it. Well, she was half-lying in it, actually. He could only give thanks she had not gone overboard. Cupping his hands around his mouth, he yelled. "Roxane! Roxane!"

Roxane scrambled to sit upright, trying to focus her eyes on the shore.

Looks like she's OK. Gesturing with his arms, Alaric yelled again. "Come in! Come on in!"

Roxane stood and waved her arms back and forth. "Alaric!" she shouted. "I'm stuck!" She wildly pointed to the boat. "I can't move the boat! Come here!" She swallowed, then coughed, trying to control her raspy voice. She'd been yelling off and on, all day long, trying to get the attention of those few families living along the cove, but the place was deserted.

It seems I'm about to play hero. "I'm coming!" Alaric made his way along the sandy shore to a neighbor's rowboat. They wouldn't care if he borrowed it. Holding the side of the boat, he took off his work boots and socks, tossed them into the beach grass and rolled up his pants. Pulling the boat over the flats and into the water, he jumped in. His smooth strokes evidenced his upbringing on Martha's Vineyard.

Maneuvering alongside the stranded boat, he tossed the line to Roxane, then placing both oars to the side, moved easily into Roxane's boat. "Hello dear. Need to be rescued by a husband in shining armor?"

"No! Well, all right, yes. But it's not my fault. The anchor is stuck," she spouted, loath to admit she needed assistance.

Alaric reached for Roxane and tilted up her chin. "Your face is burned. Your arms are beet red." He chuckled. "Like the cooked lobster look? No hat? Couldn't get to shore?"

"That's because I came out at ten this morning and have been here all day!" she cried. "I was only going to be out for an hour." Defending herself even more, she added decidedly, "I'm not a surfman's daughter for nothing. When in distress, you always stay with the ship, so don't talk to me about *shore*." She turned away.

Alaric held out his arms. "Scooch over here for a bear hug. You poor dear, being out here all day."

Roxane slid over and murmured into his chest. "It's not summer, you know. I don't need a hat."

Alaric looked amused. "Well, maybe Indian summer. But you're right. It's been surprisingly hot for this time of year. Your sunburn will fade."

Roxane moved to the bow. "Alaric, I've rowed this way, then over there. I've tried every-which way, but the anchor won't budge. Maybe it's the mud or a trap."

"Let me see." Alaric turned onto his knees and gazed out to assess the current. He tugged lightly on the anchor line. "Hmmm." He tried again from a different angle. "You're right. It's stuck."

Exasperated, Roxane blurted out, "Of course I'm right! That's what I've been telling you." She lifted a small bag and took out a knife. Holding it by the blade, she offered it to Alaric, knowing they had no money for a new rope and anchor. "Here. Cut the rope."

"No. We won't lose this anchor." He sat back down on the wooden seat, let out a deep sigh, and then unbuttoning his shirt, shrugged it off and tossed it over to the next bench.

"What are you doing?"

Alaric smiled. "My dear, the anchor is caught on something. I'm going to *un-caught* it."

"You can't! The water's freezing. It's probably fifty degrees."

Truth be told, Alaric was not looking forward to jumping in the water. He was a strong swimmer, but there's a limit when it comes to cold water. "I'm going to take a quick look." He had no choice.

"You'll catch your death." She stared at him, frowning.

He stood, then took a couple of deep breaths before diving into the murky, salt water. Some seconds later he emerged, sucked in all the air he could and went down again.

Surfacing a minute later, he shook the water from his hair, put both hands on the side of the boat and heaved himself over the side. "Brr, it's cold!"

"What did you see?" demanded Roxane as she handed him a small towel. It smelled a bit fishy, but it's all she had.

Alaric toweled his chest and hair, then grabbed his shirt. "My dear bride, the anchor was indeed stuck. I emphasize the *was* part."

"You got it loose?" She clapped her hands in praise. "Very good!"

He turned and began pulling up the anchor. "It was wedged under the French cable."

"What? You mean the telegraph cable that goes all the way to France? That cable?" She was stunned. "How could that happen? I just set out the anchor."

"The anchor was caught under it. You're going to be in big trouble when they find out you've tampered with station property."

Roxane cried out. "Like go to jail?"

"Looks like it," agreed Alaric, then added, "Just kidding."

"Don't kid me!" Roxane looked forlorn. "The anchor was under the cable. I can't believe it. I just can't believe it. Why do things like this happen to me?"

"Things like this always happen to you, like last Halloween when we were walking along. You kicked that paper bag on the sidewalk, thinking it would just sail into the air."

Roxane crossed her arms. "How would I know it had a brick in it?"

"Broke your big toe, didn't you?" He chuckled.

"Don't laugh, Alaric. Someone played a dirty Halloween trick."

"It's all right. I love it when you get into tight spots, particularly if I'm there to rescue you." He let out the line for the second rowboat and handed it to Roxane, then took hold of the oars for the smooth ride to shore. Glancing at the tin pail at the back of the boat he teased, "So, did you catch us some fish for supper or were you just ranting and raving out here the whole time?"

Laughing, Roxane snapped the towel against his shoulder. "Of course I got fish. I hunt and fish better than you!"

"Really?" Alaric exclaimed, knowing it was true.

Roxane pointed straight at Alaric and with a saucy smile added, "Go fry your own fish!"

Alaric threw back his head and laughed. "Roxane, I'm so glad you're mine. What a life we're going to have together!"

THE END

Conversation

1) Discuss the newspaper details of Roxane's 1929 wedding below and make comparisons with weddings today.

> An informal wedding party gathered at the home of Mr. and Mrs. Ernest Eldredge at Chatham, Saturday, September 14, to witness the marriage of their daughter Roxane to R. Alaric Coffin of Orleans.
>
> The bride, entering the room on the arm of her father to the strains of Lohengrin's Wedding March, played by Mrs. Gertrude Buck, was met by the groom, and the bridal party took its station in the bay window which was banked with cedars, oak leaves, and flowers.
>
> Little Miss Celestia Margaret Clark, gowned in orchid silk, acted as train bearer. Rev. Mr. Christopher of South Chatham was the officiating minister, the double ring service being used.
>
> The bride wore a gown of white satin with a veil of lace and carried a shower bouquet of bridal roses. After receiving the good wishes of the company present, the newly wedded couple proceeded amidst showers of rose petals to the dining room, which was decorated in yellow and white, and there cut the wedding cake.
>
> Under a rain of confetti within the house, the couple left shortly after for an automobile trip to Niagara Falls and Canada, the bride wearing a becoming ensemble of brown and yellow silk with hat to match.
>
> Mrs. Coffin has been a popular and successful teacher in the Beacon School at Norwood,

Mass., for the past five years and Mr. Coffin is a valued employee of the Cape & Vineyard Electric Company.

After their return from the wedding trip, they will make their home in Orleans, where Mr. Coffin has recently purchased a house [because Cape & Vineyard Electric required he live in Orleans].

The wedding gifts were in a pleasing variety of silver, linen, china, and money.[35]

Note: At this time, grooms were *congratulated*, while brides received *good wishes* and *much happiness*.

2) In the fall of 1929, when the stock market crash marked the beginning of the Great Depression, Roxane caught her own fish and started a substantial garden. (There were no catch limits governing marine fishing at that time.) Frugality was the key, wastefulness a sin, uncertainty the reality. Today, in our consumer society, people are dependent on others for food, clothing, and shelter. What can people do right now to become more self-sufficient?

3) In the blank journal Roxane was given at age 86, she recorded events that had an impact on her life. Some of those events in *The Surfman's Daughter* are seemingly insignificant like the gum left on the bench in "Saturday Treat," but all of her stories were important to her. What incidents or moments stand out in your childhood? Was there an event that changed the direction of your life, but perhaps you didn't know it at the time?

Doing

<u>Research</u>: How many miles long was the 1898 transatlantic cable called *Le Direct* from Brest, France to Orleans, Massachusetts? Find information at the French Cable Station Museum website.

<u>Research</u>: Many businesses in those days refused to hire women, a practice dating back to at least the 1880s, and a number of states had passed laws prohibiting the hiring of women in some occupations, most especially those paying higher wages.[36] When Roxane married, she had to give up teaching to become a *keeper of the home*. That said, she did assist her husband with his work, which was typical of the time. Roxane explained her role when she first married Alaric, who was employed by Cape & Vineyard Electric Company:

> "The phone would ring in the middle of the night. Lights out in Wellfleet or Brewster. We would call Ralph Battersby who worked with Alaric. While he was coming down, Alaric and I would go out to the transformer platform to load a transformer on the truck, mostly 5, 10, and 15 KVAs. The first truck Alaric had, I could shift the gears and levers, so I would sit in the cab where it was warmer and work them. Then he had a newer, larger truck and I could not shift those gears, so Alaric was in the cab and I was on the cold transformer platform. We tried so hard to get the lights or electricity on as fast as possible, but we could not please the public. They called us some very naughty names."[37]

By the 1930s, the number of laws and policies that prohibited married women from employment had increased.

When did laws and policies change? In what ways did the large increases in home prices in the 1970s make a lasting impact on the role of women workers?

Roxane's Baked Fish: Place white fish skin-side down in a greased baking pan. Top with 10–12 crumbled Ritz Crackers. If desired, dot with butter. Dilute 1 can of Campbell's Cream of Shrimp soup with some milk and pour over fish. Season with salt and pepper. Bake in a 375° F. oven for 30 minutes.

Epilogue

Family Bios through 1929

Roxane's father, ERNEST "SKIPPER" ELDREDGE (b.1874) worked fifteen years for the U.S. Life-Saving Service. His strength was evident in 1912 at the 200th Anniversary of the town of Chatham when at age 38 he won the Dory Race, competing against surfmen from other stations.[38] He's featured in the Alice Stallknecht mural at the Atwood Museum at the back of Christ's boat, manning the oars. In 1913, Skipper changed jobs to work full-time at S. W. Gould & Son, Shellfish Merchants. The year of Roxane's graduation he became partner, then later, president of the company. He also served on Chatham's Board of Fire Engineers and was elected police constable in 1920, not knowing he would be re-elected for the next twenty-one years. Known as a man of integrity, he had a quick wit and sense of humor.

Roxane's mother, MEHITABLE "HITTIE" ELDREDGE (b.1879) was married to Skipper on Thanksgiving Day 1900. She left Chatham to move to Cuttyhunk Island where Skipper first worked for the U.S. Life-Saving Service. In the summer of 1904, she, Skipper, and 22-month-old Oliver returned to Chatham. Hittie's life revolved around the daily tasks of cleaning, making clothes, and preparing food—which included feeding animals, tending the garden, and preserving food. The family attended the local Congregational Church where she volunteered in many capacities such as raising money for the Shipwrecked Sailors Fund and cooking for the 200th anniversary celebration of the church in August 1920.

OLIVER ELDREDGE (b.1902), Roxane's older brother, became that angelic choirboy his mother called him in "The Cold Fire." He died in 1915 of a ruptured appendix two weeks shy of his thirteenth birthday and was laid out to be buried from the living room of their home on Cross Street. He was adventurous, hard-working, and wise beyond his years.

ROXANE ELDREDGE (b.1904) had many amusing moments in her childhood, like the time she wanted to play croquet.[39] Balancing responsibilities and independence at a young age, she worked outside the home to earn money for the family and yet was free to roam and explore. Her volunteer activities included playing the piano for church services and banding migrating birds, and she excelled academically, receiving valedictorian honors in high school (1922) and college (1924). After teaching school for five years, she married Alaric Coffin in 1929. The next year she had her only child and named him Oliver. Spirited and energetic, Roxane had a loving heart and an incomparable gift of hospitality.

Roxane's younger brother, DESMOND ELDREDGE (b.1912) was born in the living room of the Eldredge home on Cross Street. A fun-loving young man, he began working full-time for S. W. Gould & Son, Shellfish Merchants at age 17. When he married Barbara Webster four years later, Skipper helped build a house for the couple at the back of his property, completing it in 1935. The house, at 38 Shattuck Place, still stands today and includes the barn Skipper built for his own homestead.

FARMHOUSE: Ernest "Skipper" Eldredge designed and built the big white house that is 85 Cross Street in Chatham, Massachusetts. He did the bulk of the work, including the double brick underpinning, while on leave from the U.S. Life-Saving Service during June and July 1904, with the family moving in that October, a month after Roxane was born.

In addition to the house, Skipper built the outbuildings, which included the wood shed, pig enclosure, chicken coop, out-house, well-house, and the large barn for the horse, cow, and cart. He also built the interior furniture in the house, including a lovely Welsh cabinet as a gift for his wife.

Skipper lived at the 85 Cross Street house from 1904–1964 and Roxane lived there these years: 1904–1922, 1938–1940, and 1959–1993. The family home was sold in 1998. The house still stands today.

Ernest Eldredge Homestead Barn 1904

Extra Story

A Voice that Called

*Dedicated to readers who asked for a story of Roxane
when she was older*

April, 1961 ~ Roxane, age 56
85 Cross Street House, Chatham and Cape Cod Hospital,
Massachusetts

Go see Becky.

Yes, yes. I know, Roxane said to herself. She scooped chopped vegetables into a pot, filled it half-way with water and set a lid on top. Then she reached for an aluminum pan and set cod fish neatly in the bottom of it.

Rarely did she have a moment alone these days and she was scrambling to get things done. Neighbors popped in all the time. Nieces, nephews, and grandchildren wandered in and out. Baking was always at the top of the list to keep the cookie jar filled. She glanced into the pantry just to make sure it was stocked with cranberry juice and ginger ale—a perfect combination.

Go see Becky. She felt a familiar tingle move up her legs.

"I will," she said out loud. Opening a can of Campbell's Cream of Shrimp Soup, she shook it into a bowl and whisked in a bit of milk. Then she poured it over the fish and set the pan in the refrigerator. She'd crumble Ritz Crackers over the top before baking it later that day. All was ready for when the men returned for supper.

She and her husband Alaric had moved back to the house of her childhood two years earlier to help her dad, Skipper, who was now 86. *He doesn't need a whole lot of help*, she mused. This was his forty-eighth year being a shell-fisherman and he was down at the shore every day working alongside the other men. But she was glad to help with laundry, cooking, and cleaning. Skipper had been alone now for many years.

Go see Becky.

"I will see her this afternoon." Her five-year-old granddaughter had the measles and bronchial pneumonia. The town doctor had sent her to Cape Cod Hospital two days ago. Relatives were lending a hand by taking turns staying with Becky in the afternoons while her mom worked. Roxane's shift was 2 to 4.

Becky. The voice reached into her mind and shivers started up her legs again.

She looked up and took a deep breath. "Okay, Lord. Please watch over Becky and get her fever down. I will go see her right now." She shook her head. "I guess this is what I'm supposed to do."

Roxane grabbed her coat and pocketbook. Outside, she slid into the Chevy and backed out of the driveway, the car tires crunching bits of oyster shells that made a nice, white surface. Taking the back roads, she drove the twenty miles to the hospital in Hyannis. She smiled as she thought about Becky. *She's quite the tomboy. Yes, Becky is full of it most of the time. Like the time she turned and accidently soaked me with water from the hose.*

When she entered the hospital, all was quiet. There wasn't a soul in sight. Opening the door to Becky's room, she peeked in. Becky wasn't in bed.

She scanned the room.

To the right, under a large mirror, a white, porcelain sink jutted from the wall. It was filled to the brim with ice cubes.

Sitting naked in that sea of ice cubes and slumped toward the wall was Becky. Her skin was blue. Her lips were blue.

Roxane dropped her pocketbook and grabbed a towel.

"Becky. Becky," she cried. "Look at me." Becky didn't respond. "Come to Gram. Come on." Roxane lifted her limp body out of the ice cubes with strength she didn't know she had and wrapped her tight in the towel. "Good heavens."

She marched into the hallway and yelled, "Is anyone out there? Hello? We need help here!" All was quiet. "Hello?"

Roxane turned. "We're coming here to the bed, Becky," she said in a soothing voice. "We're going to get you warmed up." Roxane knew it was common to sit a child in ice cubes to help get a fever down, but to leave a child and obviously for a long time? There was no excuse.

Sitting on the bed and holding Becky with her left arm, she unbuttoned her coat and reached around to shift a pillow to lean back on. She untucked her blouse and lifted it up to her neck. Unwrapping the towel, she pressed Becky's naked chest to her own chest, gasping as the cold hit her. She sucked in some air, shivering, and leaned back on the pillow.

Reaching down, she tucked Becky's feet in between her legs, wrapped her coat around them and scooted under the blanket. "Come on Becky," Roxane coaxed as she gently rubbed her back. "Let's get some color back. Wake up."

In her strongest, most projecting voice, she yelled toward the open door. "Is someone out there?"

Nothing.

"What we need are some hot water bottles, don't we Becky? Well, this is our little house. See how the blanket makes a house? And here we are nice and warm inside."

No response.

"You had a fever and were so very hot, but now you are way too cold." She placed Becky's hands under her armpits and kept rubbing her back to get as much heat into her as possible. "Let's get warm. Let's get warm." By this time,

Roxane's arms were aching, but she kept rubbing lightly. Grabbing the corner of the blanket, she tucked it around Becky's head.

"Dear Lord. If you sent me here, then help me. I'm not losing her like I lost my baby grandson last year." Becky's little brother had died.

She pushed back Becky's hair. "I want some color in you, dear. It was pretty miserable sitting in those ice cubes, wasn't it? But now we are warming up. And we are wondering where the nurse is, aren't we."

Becky began to move. "There, there dear. You are warming up with Gram. Gram loves you so much." Roxane rocked back and forth against the pillow.

Slowly, Becky regained some color. Roxane kept her in a great bear hug, but after a while rolled Becky off and adjusted her own clothes. She found a hospital gown, dressed Becky in it, and tucked her into bed.

After a time, a knock was heard and Becky's Uncle Dave came in for his turn to sit with her. Roxane explained what had happened. She looked over at Becky who was looking much better and kissed her on the forehead. "I love you dear. Bless your heart. You are in good hands with your Uncle Dave. Just snuggle up with him. I'll be back." She opened the door to the hallway. "A visit to the hospital director would be in order," she muttered to herself.

Later that night

Finally relaxed enough to settle in for the night, Roxane turned to her husband Alaric for a bit of pillow talk. "You believe me, right? It was the Holy Spirit who spoke to me."

"Absolutely. You listened to a voice that called. It's happened to you before." He pushed his hands through his hair. "You saved Becky."

"Do you ever wonder though? Why did the Lord take my brother Oliver? He was a wonderful boy. He'd be 58 now."

"Life's not easy."

"My mother used to say that. I realize nurses want to minimize their exposure to contagious diseases. They could catch a disease from a patient, get sick, and get their families sick. I understand their fear. I also want a hospital to be a safe place. This is a time when the whole idea of forgiveness is difficult. I don't know." She sighed. "Like I said at supper, it's obvious the nurses forgot about her."

"How did you know how to wake her?"

Roxane reflected. "You know my dad . . . working all those years in the life-saving service. Lots of times he talked of cold water rescues. And resuscitation." She yawned widely.

"You acted quickly." Alaric adjusted his pillows and pulled up the covers. "What do you always say?"

Roxane looked over at Alaric. Her eyes brightened. "You mean, *say your prayers and eat your vegetables?*"

"That's one thing, but I was thinking of *everything happens for a reason.*"

Roxane scooched down in the bed and got comfortable. "Well, may God bless everyone at the hospital." She paused. "Especially the nurses who forgot about Becky. Goodnight, Alaric."

"Good night, Roxane."

THE END

Notes

Saturday Treat

1. A surfman was one of a six to eight-member crew who worked for the U.S. Life-Saving Service (1878–1915) – the forerunner of the U.S. Coast Guard. The word "surfman" comes from the East Coast where crews launched their boats from the beaches into the surf. Surfmen were often local fishermen who were familiar with the waters and skilled in handling small boats. Their job was to save lives and property on stranded or sinking ships.

    Note: In those days, children were often referred to by their father's occupation (e.g., milkman's son). Thus, Roxane was known as the surfman's daughter.

2. Locklear. *Skipper Eldredge—The Chatham Man*, 3–6, 40–42.
    Cuttyhunk Station Keeper Log. U.S. Life-Saving Service, November 27, 1898.
    Ernest "Skipper" Eldredge's first day working for the U.S. Life-Saving Service was during the *Blizzard of 1898*, also known as the *Portland Gale*. The rescue team left at sunset in a surfboat to assist the steamship *Fairfax*, two miles offshore. Skipper remembered thinking, "My first trip and it may be my last," which reflected the unofficial motto of the U.S. Life-Saving Service: *You have to go out, but you don't have to come back*. Skipper worked full-time for these stations: Cuttyhunk 1898–1904, Monomoy 1904–1905, and Chatham 1905–1913 as a surfman. According to Roxane, "My dad . . . didn't get home very often (*Roxane's Journal*, 34)."

3. Locklear. *Skipper Eldredge—The Chatham Man*, 7.

4. Skipper and Ralph's father was Captain Oliver E. Eldredge (b.1840), who spent 26–28 years as a ship captain, then was a carpenter who repaired boats as Superintendent of the Chatham and Harwich Marine Railways, and worked for the Cape Cod Five Cents Savings Bank beginning in 1895 and rising to president from 1912–1930. Read more about him in *A Home on the Rolling Deep: The Stories of Eight Chatham Sea Captains* by Marcia Monbleau.

5. *Roxane's Journal*, 24.
6. In 1918, and possibly other years, Skipper and his brother Benjamin O. Eldredge had an extra job as ice dealers, cutting ice from cranberry bogs and ponds, keeping it in cold storage, and delivering it to residences by horse and cart for their iceboxes. (Information from Ernest "Skipper" Eldredge's Civilian Draft Registration, September 12, 1918.)
7. *Roxane's Journal*, 40.
8. *Chatham Station Keeper Logs.* U.S. Life-Saving Service, November 1909.
9. Morrow. *The New England Cookbook*, 31.

The Cold Fire

10. *Chatham Station Keeper Log.* U.S. Life-Saving Service, October 1, 1910.
11. Captain Stephen Gould (b.1838), a merchant and oysterman, started S. W. Gould & Son Shellfish Merchants in 1873. After his death, his son Benjamin Gould (b.1870) took over the business, then operated it in partnership with his brother-in-law, Ernest "Skipper" Eldredge (b.1874) beginning in 1922. The firm incorporated in 1948 with Skipper as president, then closed on December 31, 1990, having operated for 117 years.
12. *Roxane's Journal*, 25–26. The sailing to Louisiana and molasses story is retold exactly as it was written.
13. Ibid., 6–7, 34–39. This story, including not having to do wash that day, the time spent at the Gould home and Grandpa Gould asking the children to stay overnight, how they played *Puss in the Corner* the next day and the arrangement of the kerosene lamp and matches that were set on the nightstand, is described in detail. Additional information on the extent of Roxane's injuries, including a substantial, permanent hole under her armpit covered by a slap of skin, was provided by family.
14. Ibid., 6–7.
15. Ibid., 12.
16. Molasses wasn't the only food item processed by stomping. When the full-rigged sailing ship *Ladye Doris* moored at Fiume in the Adriatic Sea in 1905, Captain Charles Wood noted "low stone troughs in which barefooted boys and women were

stamping. They were treading ripe tomatoes to make tomato sauce." Hay. *I Saw a ship a'sailing*, 13.

17. Monbleau. *A Home on the Rolling Deep*, 67.

My Beautiful Pink Sweater

18. *Undocumented Times photo* c. 1991 with Roxane's explanation of her cranberry picking job.
    Roxane's Journal, 27 with explanation of working for Mrs. Laurence Howes.

19. *Roxane's Journal*, 5.

20. Ibid., 27–30. Roxane tells the story ending with, "About two weeks later I came home from school and Mother met me at the door. She had gone into my bedroom closet to get one of my dresses and the odor of rotten eggs nearly finished her off. The sweater was ruined and I had learned a real hard lesson."

Sprayed

21. Some engaged women needed to prove they could provide for a family before getting married. For example, Roxane's future daughter-in-law had to demonstrate she could cook, sew, and make a braided wool rug. These braided rugs, often made from old coats and blankets, were often either small rounds or living room sized ovals. In a letter dated December 31, 1990, Roxane writes of making another braided rug. The tradition of making braided rugs continues in Roxane's line of the family.

22. *Roxane's Journal*, 20: Halloween story.

The Pianist

23. First Congregational Church of Chatham: *The Pastoral Succession*. Reverend Jack Hyde was employed by the church from November 5, 1918 to June 29, 1920.

24. *Roxane's Journal*, 11. Roxane states, "In the first World War, I played the piano for the Navy boys church service. . . . Saturday nights they had parties and banged the daylights out of the piano. I never knew which notes were playable."

25. Locklear. *Skipper Eldredge—The Chatham Man*, 13: "At age 12, Oliver suffered a ruptured appendix and was brought to the hospital in Boston. At the time, there was no surgery for appen-

dicitis and boys around the ages of 12 or 13 were sometimes afflicted. Oliver died. Skipper spent his life in the business of saving lives and yet could do nothing to save his son."

26. *Roxane's Journal*, 11, 22–23. In this story, Roxane includes the names of the sailors' favorite hymns, when the violin string broke, their shopping trip, and the demise of the piano and platform rocker.

Notes: The Eldredge's piano was a square piano, not a spinet or upright. Also, although Roxane wrote that the shopping trip to New Bedford by train and boat was a day trip, family pointed out it was likely a three-day trip. Finally, since Roxane's family was in the oyster business, it's interesting that during the 1918 Spanish flu pandemic, oysters were hoarded due to their zinc properties that were thought to boost the immune system.

27. Ibid., 22.

Finish Line

28. Kendrick. Poem.
29. Valedictorian speech by Roxane Eldredge.
30. Ibid.
31. Ralph S. Eldredge (b.1887), ninth child of Captain Oliver E. Eldredge (b.1840) and Mehitable Eldredge (b.1842), died in 1930 – eight years after attending Roxane's high school graduation, purportedly from the effects of mustard gas after serving for 18 months in France during World War I. His wife, G. Mary Slavin (b.1888), predeceased him after seven years of marriage. They had no children.
32. Kendrick. Poem.
33. *Roxane's Journal*, 7.
34. Ibid., 1.

Out Fishing

35. "Coffin-Eldredge." *Harwich Independent*. Eight days after her marriage on September 14, 1929, Roxane turned 25 years old. (She was born on September 22, 1904.)
36. Blakemore. "Why Many Married Women . . ."

37. *Roxane's Journal*, 32–33. Like many men at the time, R. Alaric Coffin (b.1906) went into the same business as his father, Ralph W. Coffin.

Note: Ralph W. Coffin (b.1882) spent 30 years in the shipping industry (engine department) before he and his partner installed the first electric lights on Cape Cod. After working for Cape and Vineyard Electric Co., Ralph became Chief Engineer and Superintendent for Boston Edison Co. and then Chief Engineer with Lever Brothers in Cambridge, Massachusetts.

Epilogue: Family Bios through 1929

38. *1712–1912. The Two Hundred Anniversary*, 49.

39. *Roxane's Journal*, 18–19. Wanting to impress two visiting children from the city, Roxane took them to Mrs. Fuller's house to play croquet – the only place that had a set, but Mrs. Fuller wouldn't let them play. It was such a blow, the children tried to think of something to do to Mrs. Fuller. The story continues in Roxane's written words:

> John Taylor, the undertaker lived across the street. So this gang of rag-a-muffins marched over to the undertaker's and knocked on the front door. Mr. Taylor was a very tall man and wore glasses but always looked over the top of them. When he opened the door, he looked kind of surprised and said, "Yes?"
>
> I spoke up and asked, "Would you go over and dead Mrs. Fuller? She won't let us play croquet." We thought that was the worst thing we could do to Mrs. Fuller.
>
> The undertaker laughed and shut the door.

Acknowledgments, Final Thoughts

40. *Roxane's Journal*, 3.

Sources

Baisley, C. L. "Cape Cod Essays: A Chronology of Chatham Part XI."

Blakemore, Erin. "Why Many Married Women were Banned from Working During the Great Depression." *History*, July 21, 2019.

Buckley, Joseph. *Wings over Cape Cod*. Lower Cape Publishing, Orleans, MA, 2000.

Busteed, Brandon. "Why the One-Room Schoolhouse is a Vision for the Future . . ." *Education*, November 7, 2020.

Carlisle, Robert. *Beyond the Bar: The Perilous Journey*. Chatham Historical Society, MA, 2007.

Chatham Fire Department, Chatham, MA. Personal correspondence.

Chatham Life-Saving Station Keeper Logs: 1908, 1909, 1910, 1913. National Archives, Boston, MA.

Chatham, Massachusetts Annual Town Reports: 1912, 1913, 1915, 1917, 1920, 1921, 1922.

Chatham, Massachusetts High School Graduation Program, class photo, 1922. E–L Family Archives.

"Coffin-Eldredge." *Harwich Independent*, Vol. 58, No. 27, p.1, Sept. 18, 1929.

Coffin, Ralph Waldo. "Snug Harbor Obituary." NY, 1976.

Cuttyhunk Life-Saving Station Keeper Log: November 27, 1898. National Archives, Boston, MA.

Eldredge, Ernest. Civilian Draft Registration, September 12, 1918. E–L Family Archives.

Eldredge (Coffin), Roxane. High school valedictorian speech, 1922. E–L Family Archives.

—. Piano music (e.g., Academic Music Co., 1918). E–L Family Archives.

—. "Roxane's Journal." 1992. E–L Family Archives.

First Congregational Church of Chatham. Personal correspondence.

—. The Pastoral Succession.

—. "First Congregational Church" Chatham History on-line.

Grey, Spencer. "Boston to Chatham, Early 20th Century." *Cape Cod Chronicle,* December 10, 2015.

—. "The Changing Face of Stage Harbor." Unpublished.

—. "Chatham in 1916." *Cape Cod Chronicle*, June 23, 2016.

—. "Chatham Naval Air Station." *Cape Cod Chronicle*, May 26, 2016.

—. "Fires and Firefighters." *Cape Cod Chronicle.* October 29, 2015.

—. "Hurricanes that Visited Chatham." *Cape Cod Chronicle*, March 16, 2017.

—. "Ice in Chatham." *Cape Cod Chronicle*, November 24, 2016.

—. "The Train Comes to Chatham." *Cape Cod Chronicle*, December 22, 1916.

Guild, Alice Parker. "Growing Food and the Story of the Old Mill: Chatham, 1956." Orleans, MA, 1976.

Hay, Mary. *I saw a ship a'sailing.* National Maritime Museum, UK, 1981.

Hellman, Corine. "With a Chatham Flavor," 1963.

"Historical Homes: The Isaiah Lewis House." *Chatham Shopper News*, March 29, 1967.

Ives, Josephine. "Eldredge Public Library, The First Hundred Years," Chatham, MA, 1995.

Johnson, Clifton. "Cape Cod Folks." *New England Magazine*, 1902.

Kendrick, Julia. Poem written for Chatham High School Class of 1922. E–L Family Archives.

Knapton, Ernest. *Chatham Since the American Revolution.* Chatham Historical Society, MA, 1976.

Lawless, Debra. "Author Recounts WWI Attack on Orleans." *Cape Cod Chronicle*, 2016.

—. *Chatham in the Jazz Age.* The History Press, Charleston, SC, 2009.

Livingston, Eustace, editor. *The Trapper's Bible*. New York: Skyhorse Pub., NY, 2012.

Locklear, Rebecca. *Exploring the U.S. Life-Saving Service 1878–1915: 17 Student Workshops with 120 Activities*. Skaket Books and Art, 2019.

—. Personal letters from Ann Eldredge, Barbara W. Eldredge, Jan Eldredge Day (28 catalogued letters), Roxane Eldredge Coffin (38 catalogued letters plus other material).

—. *Skipper Eldredge—The Chatham Man*. Skaket Books and Art, 2017.

Manas, Joseph. French Cable Station Museum, MA. Personal correspondence.

McKay, Brett and Kate. "What is Character?" *The Art of Manliness*, June 25, 2013.

Monbleau, Marcia, editor. *A Home on the Rolling Deep*. Chatham Historical Society, MA, 1996.

Morrow, Kay. *The New England Cook Book*. Culinary Arts Press, Reading, PA, 1936.

Nason, Varney. "Chatham, Massachusetts, 1890." *Massachusetts Gazetteer*, 1890.

Nickerson, Nancy, compiler. *Cape Cod Mixing Bowl*. OES No. 91, Chatham, MA, 1963.

"A Presentation of the Transatlantic Cable and French Cable Station." French Cable Station Museum CD, Orleans, MA.

Sanderson, Melissa. Cape Cod Commercial Fisherman's Alliance. Personal correspondence.

Sheedy, Jack. "A Harwich Christmas of a Century Ago." *Cape Cod Chronicle*, December 22, 2016.

"Shipwrecked Sailors." *Chatham Monitor*, February 24, 1938.

Silva, Jared. Department of Fish and Game, MA. Personal correspondence.

Silvia, Joe. "Who Remembers . . . Star Store?" *New Bedford Guide*, December 23, 2013.

Smith, William. "Congregational Church in Chatham, 1720–1920: Historical address on the 200th Anniversary of the Church."

1712–1912. The Two Hundred Anniversary of the Town of Chatham, Massachusetts. Chatham Celebration Committee, 1912.

List of Illustrations

Front Cover, Roxane Eldredge – Rebecca Locklear

Page 10 Chatham Map 1900 – Ven Locklear, Illustrator

Page 12 Eldredge Homestead – Jack Dolan, Illustrator

1 Surfman Ernest Eldredge – Courtesy of Ernest P. Eldredge

2 Eldredge Family – Courtesy of Ernest P. Eldredge

3 85 Cross Street House – Unknown source

4 Doll Furniture – Rebecca Locklear

5 Roxane Eldredge – Courtesy of Cindy Carlton

6 Mill Hill – Courtesy of Ross Eldridge

7 Gristmill – Courtesy of Chatham Historical Society

8 Gould Home – Courtesy of Joan D. Coffin

9 Oyster River – Courtesy of Ernest P. Eldredge

10 Oyster Pond – Courtesy of Ross Eldridge

11 Eldredge Barn – Courtesy of Ernest P. Eldredge

12 Children on Fence – Courtesy of Chatham Historical Society

13 Atwood School – Courtesy of Maps of Antiquity, Chatham, MA

14 Desmond and Roxane Eldredge – Rebecca Locklear

15 Oliver Eldredge – Courtesy of Ernest P. Eldredge

16 Main Street Blimp – Courtesy of Chatham Historical Society

17 Roxane Eldredge – Rebecca Locklear

18 Class of 1922 – Courtesy of Chatham Historical Society

19 Town Cove – Courtesy of Henry Cummings and the French Cable Station Museum, Orleans, MA

20 Roxane Eldredge – Courtesy of Cindy Carlton

Page 103 Eldredge Homestead Barn – Jack Dolan, Illustrator

Three-masted Schooner, Chapter Ornament – Ven Locklear, Illustrator

Acknowledgments, Final Thoughts

On Christmas Day 1990, Roxane's niece, Barbara Eldredge Stevenson, gave Roxane a blank journal with this inscription: "I hope you'll use this to start writing down some of the wonderful stories you've told me." Roxane, who was 86 at the time, wrote in the journal from February 1991 to September 1992. The early 1900s passages from the journal became the inspiration for *The Surfman's Daughter*.

As a part of my research, Skipper and Hittie Eldredge's descendants and relatives gave interviews, provided written documents, or told stories about Roxane's escapades that were included in this book: Amy Camenga, Cindy Carlton, Nancy Eldredge Chapel, Joan D. Coffin, Joel Coffin, Oliver E. Coffin, Jan Eldredge Day, Ann Eldredge, Barbara W. Eldredge, Bruce W. Eldredge, Ernest P. Eldredge, Everett R. Eldredge, Nancy Schofield Fadely, and Barbara Eldredge Stevenson. I also had on hand Roxane's letters and other written material which provided more sources for using exact words in the dialogues.

A number of specific details about early 1900s Chatham were secured through the efforts of Amy Andreasson, Director of the Eldredge Public Library, Susan Mulgrew, a historian at the Chatham Historical Society, and Jennifer Pickett and Suzanne Martell, librarians at Brooks Free Library. Essential information on the Howes family was found by J. P. Cunniff, an archivist at the Chatham Historical Society. Chatham Life-Saving Station information and 1906 location was provided by Ross Eldridge. The Chatham map, schooner, and chapter ornament illustrations were drawn by Roxane's great-grandson, Ven Locklear, with the Eldredge homestead illustrations by Jack Dolan. Photo restoration was done by Ross Chandler Photography, Ven Locklear, and J. P. Cunniff. Details on raising chickens and homesteading came from simple living expert, Denise Berger. Recipes were developed by Dorothy Aland *(Grandma's Cobbler)*, Joel Coffin *(Hittie's Fish Chowder)*, Roxane Eldredge *(Roxane's Baked Fish)*, and Rebecca Locklear *(Family Seafood Stuffing)* with chef Alice Reader reviewing, cooking, and formally writing the recipes. My thanks to all.

I'm grateful for the support of those who read and commented on this book, particularly Cindy Carlton, John Chamberlain and the Chatham Writer's Group, Mary Krakow (editor), Grady Locklear, Celia Martin, Alice Reader (editor), and Kristine Thomas (editor). Special thanks to general editor, Chip Locklear.

Finally, I lived with my great-grandfather, Skipper Eldredge, and my grandparents Roxane and Alaric every weekend when I was young, so when I write about Roxane sliding down the banister at age six, well, I did the very same thing! And yes, that was me, sitting in the basin of ice cubes in "A Voice that Called."

I've thoroughly enjoyed this journey into the early 1900s.

> "We had no water—just a cistern, no bathroom—just an outside three-holer, no telephone, no electricity, and just a black iron stove in the kitchen which used coal and wood, but life was wonderful. People had ingenuity and independence."
>
> —Roxane, age 86[40]

About the Author

REBECCA LOCKLEAR, a twelfth-generation Cape Codder, writes history-focused, interactive, educational books and resources. She has also written and directed more than 40 productions featuring choral and instrumental music, art, dance, and drama that highlight actual historical events. An outdoor enthusiast, she can be found digging for clams, learning to drive a team of horses, or hiking *to the top*.

Books by Rebecca Locklear

The Mayflower at Cape Cod
Exploring the U.S. Life-Saving Service 1878–1915

Visit Rebecca's Teachers Pay Teachers (TPT) store for over 100 books and resources for teachers and the general public.

https://www.teacherspayteachers.com/store/
rebecca-locklear-4855

Would you like to see more photos that complement each story in *The Surfman's Daughter*? See *My Travel Research* by Rebecca Locklear on Teachers Pay Teachers.

https://www.teacherspayteachers.com/Product/
My-Travel-Research-10713374

www.ingramcontent.com/pod-product-compliance
Lightning Source LLC
Chambersburg PA
CBHW071248070526
44583CB00017B/2384